From Mourning to Morning

Healing in America's Time of Crisis

From Mourning to Morning

Healing in America's Time of Crisis

By Leo G. Frangipane, M.D.
& Gary Kunkelman, Ph.D.

A Featured Book of the Month

Executive Books
Mechanicsburg, PA

Cover Illustration and book design: Robert Miller, Art Factory

Library of Congress number 2001096888
ISBN 0-937539-59-7

Printed in United States of America
First printing October 2001

Acknowledgments

Many people had a hand in this. Bob Miller of Art Factory designed and produced the book from front cover to back literally in days – and is a great friend (still!). At Executive Books, Charlie "Tremendous" Jones provided his always-unique insights and Jason Liller led us through the jungle of "little things" that can be anything but. Joyce Piersanti has been a dear friend, unflagging promoter of this project from its inception, and source of always-excellent guidance. Our thanks to Dr. Greg Rys for sharing his experiences and insightful observations from the airliner crash in Pennsylvania.

And, of course, there are those whose ongoing love and support mean everything:
Amy, Karen, Kathy, Matt, Melissa, Michelle, Tina

*Dedicated to the families
of those who died
in the September 11, 2001 attacks*

Introduction

Pulitzer Prize-winning novelist Elie Wiesel tells of the trial of God.

He was there, witnessed it, as a young man in a Nazi concentration camp. The proceedings, grave and momentous, stretched over days as the most learned of the inmates – rabbis, sages, heads of academies – argued for and against God. Was God to blame for the horror of "the Final Solution"? Why didn't He use His power to end this consummate evil? How could God abandon the people who had pledged themselves to Him?

Evidence presented and arguments meticulously weighed, the panel of scholars and holy men solemnly announced its verdict: "Guilty as charged."

Then, the chief rabbi rose slowly to his feet.

"And now," he said, "let us go pray."

UNDERSTANDING IS something we yearn for. Yet it's so elusive. It's as if we're six-year-olds put up against a calculus book. Look and try as hard as we may, we *just don't* understand.

Never is that more so than when groping to make sense of senseless tragedy.

This modest volume doesn't attempt to explain the reasons for the violent terrorist attacks that stunned America. Very possibly, no one can. Even if we could sit the guilty parties down and compel answers, their words would likely be no more than formula condemnations that explain nothing.

This isn't about *why*, but about *how*. It looks at how we can derive meaning and understanding from what took place, and then, make that knowledge our own. It's about searching for identity – within each of us individually, as part of the nation, and as a member of the community we call humanity. In that way we can begin to find a "redeeming something" in the chaos, and use it to carry us forward.

We focus on three issues:

The first is mourning. How can we, as individuals and as a nation, move past it? How do we cope? While we mourn both privately and collectively, the solution is always personal. And importantly, events like this fit into a context, into a continuum of experience. We are a culture in mourning. We have been – differently, less acutely, but no less genuinely – for more years than we've wanted to admit.

Collectively, we have known for some time that something isn't right. As a country and as a culture, we've wrestled with this vague notion that somehow we've come off track. But we may as well have been wrestling wind. We couldn't seem to figure out how to fix it, and we couldn't stop the corrosive dissatisfaction.

People individually always find ways to try to cope, and so do people collectively. We were imaginative in our breadth, running the gamut from silly to self-destructive. We tried trips to the mall, micromanaging kids' lives, self-absorption, eighty-hour work weeks, confrontation, finger-pointing, spectacle, voyeurism, sex, drugs and a host of other palliatives. Some helped for the moment, maybe, but none were long-lived. When the buzz wore off the disease remained.

Something wasn't right. Not wanting to confront it, unable to conquer it otherwise, we grieved.

Then came the injury so unimaginably painful that none of the old answers, good or not, seemed to apply. This book suggests there *are* solutions, simple and profoundly personal.

The second issue is healing and how we can heal, as individuals and as a nation. Healing is much more than the often-painful process of coming to grips with a loss. It is a life-enhancing personal journey of understanding.

As a physician, I have come to recognize that curing the body is so much less than healing the person. In an important way, curing the body can be almost the afterthought. The way our lives are altered on a personal scale by cancer and other life-threatening ailments isn't fundamentally different from the rupture in our collective life that national tragedy brings.

I've learned that physical cures without a healing of the spirit are, at best, half-cures. I have seen that the spirit is incredibly adept at mending the body, and have come to believe that the wounded spirit facilitates and perhaps even initiates physical healing.

Any attempt to rebuild the *seen*, the physical, must draw on the unseen; sometimes, too, this unseen must be fortified and renewed. It's so in the healing art of medicine and in the healing of human suffering.

The last of the three issues actually seeks to come to grips with a question: *Is there any meaning in the senseless slaughter of the terrorist attacks?* Our answer is an unqualified *yes*. Bad times, even terrible times, are teachers. And as the best teachers invariably do, they lead us to see new things, and old things in new ways. They show us errors, and of inestimably more value, they show us possibilities. In tragedy we are given a glimpse of what can be.

This is where growth begins, and where we begin building the world that will still be ours after we pass through mourning. We're choosing now how the new world will be.

I ONCE SPENT just a few minutes that taught me all these lessons at once. It wasn't in surroundings as dramatic as triage at Ground Zero, or in the operating room removing an involved tumor. Rather, it was at a high school track.

There, six teenagers with Downs' Syndrome lined up to race. These kids were four- and five-year-olds inside, and they were keyed up in the way only kids can be. It wasn't a competition in the traditional sense, of course. The spectators had come to the Special Olympics understanding that everyone already was a winner, and the running was simply a punctuation of that.

The starter pistol fired and the enthusiastic crowd cheered and shouted encouragement. One boy – a big kid whose coordination was lacking – was maybe fifteen yards down the track when his legs became tangled. He went down in a heap, scraping elbows and knees. He sat up and began to cry. People in the stands ran to his aid.

Then the miracle came. The other five children stopped running, then calmly turned about and walked to the fallen boy. The adults moved away, as if parting on cue, and the kids helped the crying boy get to his feet. They brushed off the gravel and hugged him, and one girl kissed him on the cheek. "I hope that makes it better," she said.

Then, as the silent and stunned crowd watched, the six joined hands and walked together to the finish line. No one told them, they just knew. They responded to that part of themselves that is hard-wired for love and service in time of need.

All of us have those connections. The differences we choose to see in others are literally skin deep, or less. Coded in our genes is our ultimate connectedness to others, and with it, our potential for goodness and love, service and healing. This is our legacy, our humanity. It is also our greatest hope.

ALTHOUGH WRITTEN in one voice, this book is a collaboration from two seemingly disparate perspectives. Surgeon Leo Frangipane, M.D. – the "one voice" – is an author, healthcare consultant and nationally-known lecturer. Dr. Leo had devoted his life to under-standing healing and wellness. He has been on the front lines of the effort to make them part of both medicine and everyday life.

Gary Kunkelman, Ph.D., is a writer, university religious studies teacher and historian. His focus is the role of belief in shaping societies and individuals. Gary has explored the interplay of belief and behavior in groups as wide-ranging as Holocaust survivors, immigrants to America, and Buddhist monks.

As life so often reminds us, seemingly disparate views have a way of coming full circle, proving to be very much alike. And that is the real bedrock of this book: the differences that we think separate us are minuscule when compared to humanity's essential sameness.

Our sincere hope is that we have suggested a plan not only for moving beyond, but for moving ahead.

1

A Culture in Mourning

It has become a sad cliché that September 11, 2001, changed our lives forever. But it did.

National priorities changed in the blink of an eye. In an instant, personal lives were recast. As a nation and as individuals, we struggled to come to grips with the numbers of dead, too large to mentally absorb: not since the Civil War had America known such a killing day.

None of us could remain unaffected as we became front row observers of a terrible novelty playing out before our eyes: never had so many witnessed such vast carnage in real-time. New levels of security, and insecurity, are becoming hallmarks of everyday life for every one of us.

The tragedy also stunned in its randomness. We knew *we* could have been on a targeted flight, having a cup of coffee and worrying about making the next connection. *We* could have been walking past a targeted building on a perfect September morning, or in the elevator, or chatting with the person at the next desk as we readied for the day. We resist the urge to reduce events such as these to our solitary smallness, but ultimately, it becomes personal.

We see things so differently now. In the weeks after September 11, the magazines still on the shelves from the "old world" – the world before the attacks – seemed so trivial and self-indulgent: *Hard Muscles Fast... What he really wants you to wear... Take Ten*

Pounds Off Your Thighs... Pick Stocks Better. Others were made sadly ironic: *Crush the Competition,* or *Peace is Hell.*

We see ourselves differently, too. As the endless video clips kept replaying the tragedy for minds still resisting reality, all but Pollyannas or fools realized that our personal "business as usual" would never again be the way it was. And the changes could, in the end, prove more fundamental and life-changing than we might imagine. The terrorist attacks on America, and on each of us, may well change how we see our individual roles in our own small contexts, in the society of this country, and in the global society of humankind.

In the months before the devastating attacks, Dr. Gary Kunkelman and I had begun writing a book about healing. We wanted to talk about changes in healthcare that were shaping a new understanding of wellness. Wellness begins with *healing* – a process and a state of longevity, personal meaning, and health. Our perspectives were suddenly changed, too.

Now, with the events that began on September 11, 2001, there is so much more to talk about. Healing has become a national priority and a personal need for so very many.

How do we come to grips with something we don't even have words for? The phrases haven't yet been created, even the usually glib media grope: *You Bastards!* shouted the cover of *The Village Voice.* The *New Yorker* said nothing, its cover a page of black. In Union Square, someone had scrawled this graffiti in the dust: "I have nothing but angry words to say, so I say a peaceful nothing." It is all so amorphous. In wars before we knew without question who we were fighting and where to find them and how to go after them.

But ultimately, we do need to sort it all into internal compartments where we can start to deal with it. In our personal process of mourning we put these events in a mental box called "tragedies." Our tragedies here – there are others – go by many names and faces:

cancer, divorce, accidents, financial hardship, religious persecution, random violence, death of a loved one, vital things we failed to say or do... all these and more evoke pain.

Tragedies, no matter how devastating to the body of this planet, are ultimately something we deal with personally, inside ourselves. What we feel from the attacks on America is no less important or poignant than loss we personally feel at the death of a loved one, or the pain at diagnosis of a terminal illness. The world changes for each of us, individually, in hardship and pain. Whatever the scale, this is part of life.

And whatever the scale, the process of healing is much the same. The answers and tools for coping with a large-scale tragedy are the answers and tools that individuals successfully use to find healing, happiness and hope when confronting the bad times life deals us all.

Mourning, though, can be more than coming to grips with the hurt we feel. It is a time that offers the opportunity to discover *meaning*. Even the darkest times hold out understanding, if we'll only grab it. We mourn with our cries of grief and anger. When we stop to listen, we can hear much more.

Two things: National healing will grow from personal healing. And in the rubble we may even find our souls.

THE SHORT-FORM answer to "how to heal" is simple, and at the same time, even profound. *Healing is an internal journey of letting go of fears and embracing love.* As we learn to love ourselves and to discover who we are, something truly remarkable happens: we are much more able to love others and discover who they are.

Knowing ourselves, connecting to others: that's what it's all about.

This notion of connectedness isn't simply a dreamy, utopian notion of brotherhood. It has hard science behind it. Some of the most compelling is recent findings from the Human Genome Project. Who hasn't been awed by the incredible effort that unlocked our genetic instruction book? It's mind-boggling to consider that what makes us human, what regulates and defines us as *Homo Sapiens,* can be spelled out in a four-letter alphabet, put together by the Creator and modified by environment over evolutionary millennia.

We are such a fertile species for complexity and difference. The most out-bred population on the face of the planet, we can go just about anyplace, thrive in virtually any environment, and ultimately breed with any evolved segment of the species. We've been doing it for 75,000 years or more, since the days our Cro-Magnon ancestors vied with humanoid Neanderthals for evolutionary victory. Think of the staggering opportunity for diversity in that endless sharing of chromosomes.

But Human Genome researchers, who began work expecting to encounter countless millions of differences from one person to another, were startled at what they found.

Of the trillions of sequences our genes produce – *thousands of billions of combinations* – human beings have *less than 8,000 genetic differences.* If thousands seems many, remember the near-infinite potentialities. Yet *our differences amount to an infinitesimally tiny fragment of a single percent.* To state it positively, at the genetic level we're something more than 99.9999999% alike, and even that isn't enough 9's after the decimal.

We're alike not only in our genetic road maps, but also in our hopes and dreams, goals and desires, needs and wants. Anthropologists, sociologists, and social psychologists probing into diverse cultures and minds have shown this time and again. People who have lived abroad or traveled widely will say much the same from their life experience.

This was underscored, too – perhaps most vividly – in the aftermath of the terrorist attacks. In suffering and in countless acts of heroism and love, we saw our essential sameness, *our humanity,* so often obscured by divisions of color, ethnicity, politics or economics. People and governments around the world joined in America's sorrow and grief, again punctuating not how different we are, but how much alike. Leaders and ordinary people across the globe understood, like Ireland's President Mary McAleese, that terror knows no nationality: "This is a crime," she said, "against the foundation of our common humanity."

The common ground is there, stored in our DNA, if you will. Inside us, too, is the unique truth that belongs to each of us alone. We each comprehend infinite space for a personal journey of healing and understanding.

This journey, never an easy one, becomes all the more urgent in difficult times. At the most basic level, we don't want to hurt. That's wired into us biologically and emotionally. At a higher level, we have a longing to discover our wholeness – to *own our own personal truth.* Never is that more obvious than when bad things throw our lives out of balance.

Having lived just over half a century, most of it seeking to serve others through medicine, I've only slowly come to understand this. When illness struck my patients sought not so much a *cure* as an *explanation.* At some level they groped to understand not so much the *how* of their situations as the *why.*

But that's not the way it works. Demanding to know *why,* becoming stuck on it, keeps healing from happening. Trying to *explain* it begs the question. *Bad things happen.* That's the necessary thing to understand. At the end of the day, maybe it's *all we can* understand. We *don't know* why, and nobody has yet found a satisfactory earthly explanation. The answer may have to wait until we're face to face with God and can ask directly.

One of the things we *can know* is the personal truth that makes healing possible. We each can know our *self*. We can begin finding these when we're able to move beyond the tears and anger of our mournful responses.

For those who come to *own the truth,* the reaction to tragedy becomes not so much unanswerable questions as an axiom, an affirmation: *like joyful moments, tragic moments have meaning when they permit us access to our personal identity... access to our personal truths.*

"In the depth of winter," wrote Albert Camus, "I finally learned that within me there lay an invincible summer." Even life's darkest moments teach... *especially* life's darkest moments. And that is where the healing begins and ends. From the seeds of the worst, the fruits of life's best can blossom.

The Eastern religions offer a perspective on life that is especially relevant in bad times. The world, they teach, is *the way it is,* not the way we want it to be. Are we going to change the world, reshape it to accommodate us and our wants? Of course not. Their solution is not to squander energy trying, for there's more important work to do.

They teach that there *is* a place where our will is absolute, where our ability to work change is unhindered. It's within each of us. We can always change our *self,* and how we respond to the world – whatever it may deliver. And as Eastern teachings so often are, this one is wrapped in a wonderful irony: *no one person can change the world, but he can change himself. As people change themselves, they find they have changed the world.*

ISN'T IT SOMEHOW untoward, if not plain selfish, to think of oneself when tragedy strikes? After all, it's bigger than *just me.* Others have suffered so much more.

It *is* bigger, and others *have* suffered more, and we *do* need to think of ourselves. It's necessary, not selfish, and wariness of our feelings is a very human reaction that reveals our ultimate connection with others. Healing, though, is personal, not corporate. It is all about addressing the hurt *I* feel. Others can help us heal, but they don't heal us. We heal ourselves.

As thinking beings – *rational animals* – we spend our lives paying attention to what goes on around us. We try to be attentive, to experience and understand our part of the world. Most of us are pretty good at it... at least, we think we are and do our best. I've tried to mostly kept my eyes and mind open, and my mouth shut. The trouble is, I was well into the game before I realized I had it all wrong. I was focusing on the wrong place: I was looking outward instead of inward.

Like journalists, anthropologists, auto mechanics or detectives, doctors are trained observers. The finest nuance, the most subtle physical sign of disease or illness, ideally lays itself open to the skilled healer's notice and interpretation. That's how I was trained. So much medical training focuses on these skills that you might expect the really successful doctor be the consummate problem solver. Many are, indeed. Ideally, that's as it should be.

But as happens, an all-consuming emphasis *here* more often works to shortchange *there*. Balance, by whatever name we might call it, is always a goal in life, even a necessity. Yet it's *so* elusive; if life were a tightrope, we would spend most of it in the net. Other-focused, highly analytical medical training and practice give short shrift to personal mindfulness. There's *never time*.

I'm not suggesting that doctors are the only ones afflicted. The ill is endemic. We're a nation of mental joggers, always running, and we can't seem to find the place where we're allowed to finally stop to rest and regain energy. It's there, the resting place, *but where*?

We all see what we're conditioned to see, whether from years of training, deep-seated convictions or the sensory input we're constantly bombarded with. The last of those, particularly, may work to supersede even such strong life influences as training, belief and family. The sensory images continuously beamed at us speak anything but softly, and always carry a big stick. They are ubiquitous and overwhelming. No wonder we can't see things in front of us.

As the disasters unfolded on September 11 we sat glued to our televisions. We saw, but couldn't comprehend. Over and over, we numbly watched the same video loops of crashing planes and tumbling buildings, and strained for the freshest bit of news. We needed, as individuals and as a people, to confront our disbelief, to come to believe it happened. That always is the first stage of mourning.

Something that many people remember vividly is how *unreal* it was. It even looked like a movie apocalypse that Hollywood might have staged. *"You're kidding,"* was an almost knee-jerk response to first hearing the news, allowing us to hope for another second it was some horrible joke. For mornings to come, in the waking seconds when the unconscious and conscious meet, we would wonder momentarily whether it hadn't all been just a nightmare, and this would be another beautiful September day. Seeing the terror replayed again and again, we *had to* believe. We finally had no recourse but to accept the evidence of our eyes.

Yet days later, with new information scant, we were still there, fixed by the broadcast images. People told themselves, and you could overhear them telling others, how depressed they were seeing the tragic events over and over. The simple solution was to say, *Stop! Enough! I've got to step back.* Few of us could. We were trying to understand.

There *is no* satisfactory way to explain it or understand it. Evil, especially consummate evil, is incomprehensible. The utter senselessness completely confounds us. Unable, even in our wildest dreams, to conceive of ourselves as author of such terrible evil, we can't "go there." Unable to process it in our consciousness, we can never explain it – not to ourselves or anyone else, at least not in a way that truly convinces.

Realizing that is a part of what maturity is about. A child asking her father why the sky is blue sees maturity as knowing the answers. When we're no longer children, we realize we don't even know most of the questions... and that many of the important answers must always remain open-ended. Understanding that, we can mourn and begin to heal.

WITH THE WISDOM of looking backwards – Monday morning quarterbacking – we could see signs of what came to be on September 11. Osama bin Laden had boasted to an Arabic-language newspaper in London, just weeks before, that he had planned "very, very big attacks against American interests." The word even flashed around the internet that Nostradamus had predicted it, although that was just one bit of the avalanche of bogus internet information.

Ironically, on September 10, Congress received a voluminous report from a task force on terrorism. It warned of just such a large-scale attack and the nation's ill-preparedness to deal with it, just as had previous government commissions on terrorism. If only Congress had.... If only the FBI had.... If the CIA had.... If the person at the car rental desk just had... Or if only, as two well-known TV preachers intoned, *if only* the humanists and liberals and gays and lesbians *hadn't*.... Some people beat themselves up, some beat up others as a way of trying to construct understanding, although both are often unjust and usually unproductive.

We don't feel safe any more. And that is an egregious loss. It's new territory completely. Foreign observers call the September 11 attacks "the end of America's innocence," the terribly wrong conclusion to our happy-ever-after belief that our soil is a safe haven. It's scary. We wonder if, and where, it will happen again. To some it's apocalyptic. "We have just witnessed the opening battle of the Third World War," announced an essayist in the Canadian news magazine *Maclean's*. Being scared isn't good, but it's not irrational, either.

Our fear is greater now, sure. But going back to the *old world* before September 11, did we really *feel safe* then? We've been scared, I think, for a long time. Threats and insecurities have now been heaped onto what was already a threatening world. In the old world we knew in our collective gut that something was wrong. If we ever began to wonder, "Is it just me?", we soon were assured not. There was always a pollster quantifying our overwhelming conviction that somehow we had gotten seriously off track.

We were scared and perplexed by random acts of violence that snuffed out the lives of schoolchildren, people at work, couples sitting in a fast food place. We had grown afraid to walk our own city streets. Always, there was some new "rage" to read about – road, airline, grocery store, stadium. Rudeness, self-absorption and "getting mine" had become operating principles.

We had begun to again become anxious for our jobs, perplexed and angry that CEO's earned seven-figure bonuses for putting workers on the street. The people we had elected to lead seemed to be failing badly, showing themselves as little more than crude cartoons of pettiness and divisiveness.

Most poignant of all, perhaps, was how old people talked about *how it used to be*. How *could they* speak about the Depression and World War II, and then, in the next breath, say "things were better then"? Sure, some of it was the nostalgic cleanup that often goes with looking back, but there was clearly more to it. We sensed and feared that our community was crumbling.

We had already become a culture of mourning. We knew we had lost something important, we grieved and feared for what was happening and what we were letting ourselves become. As individuals – fear, too, is ultimately personal – we handled it in our own ways.

My fear came out in restlessness, and I was almost in my fortieth year before I came to understand it. By then, I hardly knew who I was. I worked hard, yet seemed to lack direction. Spiritually, I was excellent at mouthing the phrases, but bankrupt when it came to embracing and living the meaning.

You find ways to handle it, or try. At first I consumed myself in work. After all, for a young surgeon whose star was ascending, that was the perfectly acceptable thing to do. When work didn't consume enough hours – there were some times, no matter how well I planned – I could always buy toys to keep me occupied.

In the end it would cost me a marriage, beloved friendships, and almost, my children. I came to finally understand that I was grieving, mourning, for the empty shell I had let my life become. Only then I realized what I always knew, and would have heard if I had only listened: this subconscious sorrow could not be drowned in a sea of *things, other people or activity.*

And I came to realize, too, that my predicament was shared by too many others. Years have passed, and I never stop being astounded at how many tell me their same feelings. For all of America's opportunities, for all of our material wealth, for all that is fundamentally right about our society and ourselves, we have been creating people bankrupt of self... people who measure their treasures in any way that keeps them from taking a deep, hard and honest look at themselves.

In ourselves is *exactly* where meaning and understanding are hidden. Religions all say as much, and philosophies, and even popular culture. I'm reminded of the movie *Contact,* adapted from a Carl Sagan book. The heroine is a scientist consumed with the possibilities of life elsewhere in our universe. In the climax, she is counseled by a benevolent and wise alien. "You are a marvelous and restless species," he begins. "You seek to know answers light years away from where you come. Yet the answers to all your questions about God, life and creation are inside you."

The alien got it right. And tragedy, we find, underscores the importance of finding what is true.

JOHN SNYDER, NINTH degree black belt, is America's highest-ranking practitioner of Okinawan Kempo karate. Even if you didn't know he was a karate master, he's not somebody you'd want to square off with in a barroom brawl. He's towering guy, and with his beard and the braid that trails down his back, a quick first look might say bouncer, or biker – actually, he is a Harley enthusiast.

When you talk to Master Snyder, you quickly see that he is one of the most gentle of men. Many of the best martial artists are. The most important karate skill, he tells his students again and again in dozens of different ways, is stepping back. Here is always the best way to defuse a threatening situation. Moreover, whatever the situation may lead to, you give yourself the moment to see clearly.

Stepping back is something we seldom do, even in best of times. Or rather, *especially* in the best of times. We've become victims of sensory assault most days of our lives. Call it *battered consumer syndrome*, if you will, for we are consumers not only of things, but of information. And information is perhaps the biggest club. It's *all the time*: talk shows, news reports, politicians, infomercials, ads, "official spokesmen," dueling experts, celebrities, con artists, screaming radio hosts, TV preachers, pitch men for causes and groups of every description... all vie for our attention as they sell their goods, ideas, biases, philosophies or brands of "reality" in our material world.

We wake up with the radio, start the day with a newspaper or maybe TV, grab earphones to jog, drive to work with something playing, answer the phone in the office and the cell phone when out, page through a magazine, send a raft of email messages and get even more, answer calls from telephone marketers at dinner, migrate to the TV as soon as we're sated, log onto the internet, read a few pages in bed or maybe switch back to the TV as we're falling asleep. Then it starts all over. No doubt one of our next "advances" will be a system that allows us to connect to some information stream while we're sleeping – after all, can we really afford to squander six or seven hours of every twenty-four?

The result is that we spend inordinate amounts of our waking time and energy, mental and physical, taking in and processing it all. We're good, but not limitless. Like a sponge, we ultimately reach a saturation point. And like a sponge, we sop up whatever we're presented, good, bad or indifferent. Considering how much is filed under "bad" or "indifferent," we end up being awfully busy absorbing nothing.

Compare that to the amount of time we spend absorbing information about the person we spend 100% of our lives with. That, of course, is your *self.* Could it really be we've signed onto a world where we're too busy to know ourselves?

If your childhood was like mine, animal stories were a favorite way of teaching character traits. Many of us learned about the constant tortoise and the too-cocky hare, the industrious ant, wise owl, and of course, brave and faithful Lassie, who never tired of Timmy's gift for getting into ridiculously bad situations.

One of the earliest images I recall is the busy squirrel, that bushy, nose-to-the-grindstone workaholic whose moral was "save up for the winter." That's the trick, stay busy, save for a rainy day. It was a letdown years later to learn industriousness has nothing to do with it. A squirrel is on a perpetual quest for acorns because he has more energy than brains. The animal doesn't have the foggiest where he's planted all those nuts he devotes his life to gathering. He can't own the acorns he doesn't know he has. Moreover, he can never get off the treadmill he creates for himself. A lot of us would feel right at home as squirrels. We get stuck, and can't seem to get unstuck.

The books of the Sufi are filled with the most wondrous

instructional stories. One of my favorites is about a holy man, a mullah, who comes upon a friend. The man's combing the ground in front of his house, apparently looking for something.

"What are you doing?" asks the holy man. "Why are you on your hands and knees when it's not prayer time?"

"I lost my house key and can't find it," the friend replies, rummaging among the flowers.

The mullah offers to help, asking where he should begin his search.

"I lost my key in the *house*," the man replies.

The mullah is certain his friend has been too long in the hot sun.

"In the *house*? Are you *mad*? How do you explain crawling around in this yard like an infant, searching for a key you lost inside?"

"For the best of reasons," the man explains. "There's more *light* out here."

It becomes so easy to get stuck, like the man who lost his key, searching in the wrong place. It becomes easy, even obvious, to seek answers to life's critical questions in the light of what the world shows us.

We seek out answers in the usual places, and sometimes come away with a perspective we think might help. Sometimes it *does*, although seldom for long. If we had the ultimate system, supplement or seminar, the flourishing self-help industry would grind to a halt.

The Sufi parable challenges us to look in the right place. Even more, it challenges us to be mindful of who we are. To truly discover the key to our lives, the story preaches, go where the solution can be found. Getting there needn't be a pilgrimage to a holy shine, or climbing to the top of a mountain to sit at the feet of a sage. We don't even need to pack a carry-on bag, because answers are *inside each of us*.

The irony, though, is that the shortest trip can be the longest.

When we look around, we find an abundance of things and activities that help cocoon us and keep us from going *there*. Stay busy enough, diverted enough, and we stay at the saturation point, unable to do or take in any more. True, that's a sort of equilibrium, but beyond that, being a sponge doesn't have an awfully lot to recommend.

Why not just stand up and declare, in a line straight out of the movies, *"I'm sick of it, and I'm not going to take it any more!"* God knows we've all wanted to.

Well, I think part of it is that the devil we know is usually preferable to the devil we don't. We don't like the dark, and for all we know, that's what we'll find inside. We're naturally wary of unexplored places – a concern we're particularly conscious of now. One consolation is that reality is rarely as bad as our fears. Yet uncharted territory has always been a place where fears can take root and grow. The unknown expanses are the perfect environment for unimaginable terrors to dwell. The old mapmakers knew as much when they populated unexplored seas with monsters, and engraved in bold letters across unmapped lands, "Here be dragons."

As a nation we've stepped off into a great unknown, and there may, indeed, be dragons. If that is an overwhelming notion, understand that it *should be*. None of us is equipped to micro-manage the macro-reality of our world. *Go to where the answers can be found.* The key is lowering our sights and focusing, and in so doing, upping our chances of making a difference.

We heal when we know ourselves. Healing begins not at some global or institutional or systemic level, but in ourselves – from our own centers. Obvious, yes, and seldom simple. Like any, *our own* unexplained places scare us, we avoid them; we keep out of imagined harm's way and spend our lives taking the long way around. We're stay-at-home explorers who won't even untie our ship from the piling. We fear that if we do, we'll drift over the edge.

While we demand answers to the unanswerable, we overlook the even more important questions that we *can* answer by going inside. We never will get at them unless we act. What continents will we never discover? What sights, what treasures, what new worlds will ever stay hidden? It's the journey of a lifetime, literally, that's ours to take.

Begin by understanding rationally, if not emotionally, that dragons aren't a flourishing breed, even in *terra incognita*. Always, monsters we fear we *might* encounter are vastly more terrible than the ones we do. Once past these dragons of our making, we can begin to uncover the light of our being; and doing that sets us on the path to completing our personhood.

TEACHERS TELL HOW they learn from their students, and parents from the child. Doctors learn from their patients. Bill was one who taught me.

It's common to have older patients in a medical practice, so I wasn't at all surprised when the seventy-six year-old man walked into my office. I hadn't expected that he would introduce me to his father.

Bill Reifsnyder was ninety-nine-years-old, and that day, didn't look well. I found out he had lost twenty pounds recently, was severely anemic, and had a softball-sized mass in the right lower quadrant of his abdomen, a cancerous colon tumor. As gently as I could, I outlined to Bill and his family the diagnosis, course of treatment and the frankly iffy prognosis.

I finished and asked him how he felt about what I had said. Physically weak but obviously sharp and alert, the old gentleman responded, "Let's get on with it! I still have a lot of living that I want to do."

Bill was soon in the hospital, prepped and ready for surgery. Our next encounter, in the operating room, was the most significant event of my professional life. Bill was facing a huge procedure here, and at his age, simply surviving surgery would be a minor miracle. Nobody had missed that fact, including the patient.

I play music for patients, or even sing for them in the OR. The operating table is truly a scary place, but it can also be a sacred and holy place of healing. Much as music has its place in our churches and shrines, so does it have a place here, although any singing of mine would hardly qualify as angelic.

This particular day I was wracking my brain trying to find a CD that I thought Bill would like. Short on good ideas, I finally decided on the oldest living male vocalist I could think of – at that time, Frank Sinatra.

Old Blue Eyes was crooning from a boom box in the OR as we wheeled Bill in. He wasn't shy with his opinion: "I hate this music!" was the first thing he said. As I tried to find out where I went wrong, he held up his hands in a time-out and said, "No, no, I like Sinatra just fine. I can't stand this song."

"What do you mean?" I asked.

"Listen to what's playing."

I stopped for a moment to catch the words: *All of me...why not take alllll of meee....*

With the operating room in an uproar of laughter, a nurse grabbed a new CD off the pile and popped it the player. When she hit *play*, there was the Four Seasons: *Let's hang onnn, to what we got....* She swears to this day, and I've held her feet to the fire many times since, that it was a totally random pick.

There are, it seems, no coincidences.

I often hold a patient's hand as they go off to sleep. I find it centering for me and helpful for them. I want the patient to know they have an advocate on the other side of the scalpel. As I did – Bill was being anesthetized – he looked at me with his pale blue eyes and said, "Doc, don't be so hard on yourself. There's only one healer."

That was it. Bill had shown me what I was struggling to find, the true role of physician: to be the conduit of healing, not the cause... to be a channel for love and healing grace.

There's more to the Bill story. I'll always remember walking into his hospital room a couple days later and seeing him sitting placidly in bed, chewing. A nasogastric tube, taped in place to keep his stomach empty, ran to the wall suction. On his table was a half-eaten hoagie.

I couldn't believe what I was seeing. My mind was racing, *how many of his stitches has he burst with this antic?*

"Where did you get it and why are you eating it?" I demanded.

"I'd rather not say," he responded calmly, "and because I was hungry."

How could you be angry with the guy? The sutures held, Bill and I were lucky. I've always believed he *knew* the stitches would be fine when he plotted to have the sandwich sneaked in.

By day five in the hospital, when a patient normally begins to sip liquids and take the first tentative steps out of bed, he was strutting up and down the hall, a student nurse on each arm. He needed the cane he was using, but the young nurses were pure icing. I told Bill he may as well go home, as he clearly had no need to be hospitalized longer. He let out a whoop and started packing.

Like his hospital stay, his recovery took half the time you would expect for a healthy young person, let alone a man zeroing in on the century mark. I was eager to see what made Bill tick, so I asked him when he came in for an office visit. Bill was certainly ready to tell me.

He pulled up his trousers and snapped his suspenders over his shoulders, assuming a stance that would have done justice to a nineteenth century orator delivering a dramatic reading. He clearly had done this before.

"First," he said, holding up a single finger, "it's important to go fishing every day. If possible, eat what you catch. You know, God does not count against you the days that you fish, so I'm really only eighteen."

A second finger went up.

"Always have both short and long term goals. Do something you have to do and also do something you like. But don't have too many goals, 'cause you'll never get anything done.

"Finally," he announced as the third digit rose – his eyes were bright with a mischievous twinkle like you sometimes see in a ten-year-old – "the most important of all: surround yourself with people who keep their minds full and their bowels empty."

A dozen psychiatrists would have struggled to come up with a better plan, and probably not succeeded. At the most basic level, Bill's philosophy requires an understanding and acceptance of who and what we are. He *understood*. He made the very best of what he had been given. He understood completely the importance of balance, and not being overwhelmed by "what you have to do." He knew who to avoid – and I always especially liked the way he said it. He knew about stepping back, and the importance of purpose.

I thought of him not long ago as a firefighter at Ground Zero was being interviewed.

"You've been working here around the clock for weeks when all hope is gone," said the on-camera face dramatically. "Brother fire-fighters perished, yet to a man, your spirits are good. How can that be?"

The fireman didn't need time to think.

"We have a purpose for being here," he answered, "just like we have a purpose for going to work every day. We have a job to do."

Bill, by the way, died at the age of 104. His funeral was a celebration of life.

I heard that he went fishing until just a few days before he died. If he were still around, I'm sure he would advise it now.

THE CHINESE, WITH their pictographic language, have a unique way of making a point: they combine words to make new words, and often they'll teach a lesson while conveying a meaning. The Mandarin word for *crisis* is one of those. It links two other words: the words for *danger* and *opportunity*. To the Chinese a crisis is a *dangerous opportunity*.

To us, at this particular point in time, danger is obvious. It has become a fact of our lives that we recognize vividly. We don't know when or if it will lift. Life has never been in the habit of telling us what is around the corner. The danger part of the crisis we have, like it or not.

The one possible redeeming act, it seems to me, the act that brings some meaning to this incomprehensible event, is to seize the opportunity. The opportunity is to see who we are, and where we're going. We have everything to gain... including even what we've lost along the way.

2

Moving Within

In their shocking suddenness, tragedies challenge us to take the long view. They are lenses that help us see our lives in perspective.

"Without vision," the holy books of the Jews and Christians teach, "the people perish." Vision, when keen and focused, is the parent of action. Visualize the world you want to live in. Then make it happen. To a larger extent that we might ever imagine, we *can* do that for ourselves. We look back when we mourn. Moving through mourning, we look ahead.

What we choose to do, or perhaps agree to do, becomes a central part of our reality. A modern-day philosopher named Christopher Losch suggests that each generation is plagued by its own peculiar pathology. Ours, he says, is *"hurry sickness."* I think he's right. We're always running to keep up, to get it done, to be here or there. More and more, that's not even to get ahead, but to stay in place.

As late as the mid-1800's, an intelligent person could aspire to know everything about everything. A tall order, yes, but not a patently ridiculous idea. At the very least, an "educated man" was expected to have a broad knowledge that skipped across boundaries and drew from many wells.

People like Thomas Jefferson and Ben Franklin are prime examples. Statesmen, ambassadors, inventors, scientists, professional men, gifted writers, tireless civic promoters – *what didn't they do!* Both were exceptional, sure, but the span of their knowledge was not necessarily exceptional among men of "their class."

Today, of course, it's inconceivable that one person could know everything about *anything*. Medicine, chemistry, jazz, world affairs, literature, the human mind, major league baseball – crack any of them into a hundred or more parts, and then *maybe*, by constant application, a person *might* become expert in one small, cordoned-off piece.

The body of information in our age, it's claimed, doubles in about five years. What was gospel yesterday is often heresy tomorrow. Professionals, academics and researchers could spend all their waking hours just keeping up with new developments in their fields. Those of us of "a certain age" look back in awe at how things have changed since we started doing our jobs. Whether you're auto mechanic or surgeon, soldier or politician, little is like it used to be.

In a supercharged world, ultimate truths are often the simplest and unchanging. Hope, love, service, faith, courage – these all remain fixed and steady among the movable feasts on our life calendars.

At times we'll think they're outmoded or broken. We may even think we've lost some of them completely. But sooner or later, they come around and deliver a good whack to announce they're still around and doing fine, and we wonder how we could have been such fools for so long. Which is humbling, maybe, but *very good* news. These are the tools that challenge and help us grow.

To access them, to make them our own, we never have to look far. At our centers, in some infinitesimally small place in this fabulous container we call ourselves, our answers are stored. They simply wait to be found. Yet even if we accept that, why choose times like these, when we're already emotionally occupied? Who feels like starting some deep interior journey *now*?

Two thoughts: One, there is never a better time for self

examination and exploration than bad times, as I hope to explain. Two, there is always life after mourning.

MOURNING CHALLENGES us to understand its lessons, it shouts them at us, sticks them right in front of our eyes... and sometimes, we'll even get the message. The important thing, after mourning, is what has always been important: what we make of our lives.

In the aftermath of the terrorist attacks, as so often when bad things happen, a window opened. This observation window is seldom tall or wide, and how long it might remain open is anyone's guess. History's evidence, though, suggests not long.

Through it we can clearly see *possibilities*. We've been given a picture of what *can be* if we will make it so.

In between the terrible images of collapsing buildings, crashing airliners, and the tear-stained faces of the hurt and hurting, we have been privileged to see humanity at its most noble.

We have seen an outpouring of love and caring on a scale that most of us have never witnessed. We have seen people connecting to each other as *people,* and the "impenetrable" barriers of race or status or ethnicity simply evaporate. We have seen selfless leadership and cooperation in a society where contentiousness and divisiveness and cheap confrontation have so long been the norm.

In the midst of so much pain and uncertainty, we have seen the extraordinary – *how can that be?* It's as if we've filtered out the grays and have been left with the black and white. We see, and I don't know what the right word is, but *perfection* comes to mind, and doesn't sound completely ridiculous. We see the extremes of our reality: the best of the human spirit juxtaposed against the foil of humanity's worst.

When we see so many lives cut short, such random violence, we automatically start to sort out trivial from essential. The bad times remind that life is far too precious to rush through in a way that demeans what we truly hold dear.

We relearn that human connections are too vital to have them broken by the conceit that differences outweigh similarities. With eyes that only tragedy gives, we are given the opportunity to reexamine and recast priorities. *Focusing on what can be* is a powerful tool for getting beyond mourning and beginning to heal.

THINGS THAT WE "don't get" sometimes become clear when seen through the eyes of other cultures and peoples. The ancient Hindu religion, I believe, can tell us much about focus. The Hindus teach that in the quest for understanding, a person will live thousands, perhaps millions of lives in numerous life forms. Despite the many shells each soul will wear on its journey, the truths at its center are unchanging. "The traveler may be slow," the Hindu holy men counsel, "but God is not in a hurry." The journey goes on and on, they believe, until the traveler "gets it right." Doing that starts with peering inward, recognizing the divine spark within, and then, using it to direct and focus life.

To bring ourselves into focus, we can cultivate *the habit of peering inward* through our own lenses. *Habit* is a key word: there is genuine power from making an everyday thing of focusing on yourself. This can be confusing, I've found, particularly if the listener emphasizes *peering* and skips past *inward*.

Focusing on ourselves doesn't mean the ritual we're most accustomed to: looking in a mirror. After all, that doesn't tell us much, certainly not much that most of us care to dwell on. Our body stares back, too flabby, with less hair and more wrinkles than we would like. We tsk-tsk at what we see, take a shot at mentally making the best of what's there, and move on. Or maybe, if we're feeling especially motivated, we'll vow to cut down on the Eskimo Pies and start jogging again.

As brief as the daily ritual of peering in the mirror is for most of us, those few seconds are usually many more than we routinely take to look at what's *truly* important. Taking that look, *the look inside*, is vital. It's critical, it's must-do, there's no skipping it. *In here*, inside, is where the truly important stuff waits to be found.

Dr. Deepak Chopra, the Harvard-trained internist with an interest in integrative medicine, says that the center of our health, our wellbeing, is right behind the breastbone. He's not referring heart or lungs or anything an anatomist could identify, but rather, to our understanding and capability to love.

My friend Charlie Metcalf taught me that lesson many years ago. C.W., as he likes to be called, is a humor therapist and a former screenwriter for the TV show *Happy Days*. C.W. was working with patients at a Texas burn unit when he met a twelve-year-old who had been horribly burned and disfigured.

The story was tragic. In a drunken, abusive attempt to teach this youngster not to play with matches, his father poured alcohol over him and set him on fire.

C.W. tells how this child had spent most of a year in a hospital with deep second and third degree burns of the head, face, neck and chest. He had undergone dozens of operations to try to make him recognizable as human again. Despite the surgical teams' almost heroic efforts, the child was terribly scarred. His ears were burned off, a lifeless eye looked melted over, he had a prosthetic nose and a little slit where his mouth used to be. Even after all the reconstructive surgery, most of us in, natural revulsion, would unthinkingly turn away... or worse, stare.

Because his wounds ran deeper than flesh, a psychological support team was part of his care. Their job was to ready him to confront the outside world head-on. Before he could do that, though, it was vital he meet *himself* head-on. One of his nurses had an idea: *maybe looking at himself in a mirror could help him come to an acceptance of himself.*

And so it was done. A full-length mirror, the kind they use in clothing stores, was brought to his room. Each day he would stand in front of it for five minutes, wearing only his Power Ranger briefs, looking at himself.

Try it, five minutes in front of a mirror. You find that a mere 300 seconds can be a very long time.

Each morning the burned boy would push his IV pole over to the mirror and stare, not moving his gaze. After several days the child still hadn't offered any clues about what he was thinking and feeling, so they asked him: "What do you see when you look in the mirror?"

Children are pure, often still unaffected by things that would make adults scream. They figure out problems in a simple and honest manner that can teach a wondrous lesson to those of us who are no longer children.

"I look into the mirror and I see me," he said. "And then I look into the mirror and I see *me!*"

Terribly disfigured, with physical and psychological pain greater than most of us will ever be called on to bear, he could see what was his alone. The *me* inside was still there, and always would be... true, hopeful, faithful and loving.

AN AWARENESS OF *me* is an elusive commodity. It speaks to an important need that goes unrecognized too often, swept over by the business and hurry of life.

Our culture orbits around *things,* and that makes it awfully tough to get hold of the invisible within. We're implicitly asked all the time to question its worth, and then, to register our answer by ignoring it. After all, what we have inside can't be sold at a profit, packaged with a logo, or put out for neighbors to see... so the temptation is to ask – without really asking – *what value can it really have?*

The value is beyond price. Intimacy, the kind that leads to self-discovery and true realization of identity, is a marvelous healing tool. Intimacy with our *self* can cure the body, mend the mind, and salvage the soul. Others have memorably defined intimacy this way: *into me I see.*

Intimacy is about *love.* Even the toughest-sounding, most hard-bitten of humans shares the need to love himself and others. Particularly to those who have grown up in the image of the taciturn, self-reliant cowboy, whose only true love is his horse, that can be an uncomfortable idea. When I was growing up, "loving yourself," or hearing somebody say you did, would have been the stuffings of a knuckle sandwich... and this from a romantic Italian, no less.

Self-love isn't something we're taught to do or value. Actually, we Americans have always been extraordinarily tough on the idea – historians trace this facet of the national character all the way back to the New England Puritans. It's our nature to believe self-love is too narcissistic, somehow untoward, too self-possessed. As one observer has wryly noted, how different things might have been if Plymouth Rock landed on the Pilgrims instead of the Pilgrims landing on Plymouth Rock.

So we search outside instead. Wear the right logos, adore the latest pop icon, drive the right imported motorcar, eat and drink the trendiest of consumables. The message is reinforced hundreds of times each day. *Buy this and you'll look great, feel great, get great dates.* We do and still don't feel any better, our looks haven't improved, and neither has our love life. We can't buy intimacy any more than we can buy belonging.

We *can* find those things in our selves.

A venerable Buddhist abbot was asked to explain how this most selfless of religions could teach self-love. He answered simply: "Unless a person first loves himself, it is impossible to love others." It *is* as simple as that.

The religions of the East don't have a lock on this wisdom. We know the Christian admonition to *love your neighbor,* but what of the next part we so easily pass by: *as you love yourself.* You can't love others until you love yourself. That love has to come first.

I've witnessed people facing their imminent death who have taken stock and realized that loving themselves is the path to true wellness, to healing. Looking inward, understanding your own self worth, and practicing it daily can be a path to explosive growth. You'll find any number of tools readily available to quiet the spirit and open ourselves *to ourselves.*

Herbert Benson, researcher and physician at Harvard Medical School, talks about becoming "stress hardy" by tapping into a built-in mechanism we each possess. This is the famous *relaxation response.* It's sitting quietly, perhaps listening to soothing music, counting breaths and emptying the mind of peripheral stimuli. Doing this faithfully actually produces measurable body changes, such as lowering pulse rate and blood pressure and slowing brain wave activity. Not measurable, but also reported most of the time, are "feelings of peace and calm."

It has been accepted wisdom for some time that our frenetic lifestyles set us up for stress-related illnesses. The *catecholamine response,* the release of adrenaline-like substances from adrenal glands in response to our sense of worry and hurry, constricts blood vessels, speeds up heart rate and increases anxiety.

Benson's simple exercises help turn these hormones off for a while. Soothing calm replaces angst and agitation. Scientists call it biofeedback, and it can be used to relieve pain and other noxious feelings as well as anxiety.

Another method that "works" is TM, or transcendental meditation (or what my friend Greg Schweitzer of the Mind-Body Center calls "effortless meditation"). This is the meditation that, helped along by the Beatles' pilgrimages to India, earned prime space in magazines and on college campuses in the 1960's and 70's. There are things from that era we've thankfully discarded, but TM shouldn't be lumped with bellbottoms. Psychologists sometimes teach a stress-control technique much like it, but packaged differently, as "therapeutic meditation."

In practice, these forms of meditation aren't markedly different from the relaxation response. And here, too, scientific studies demonstrate their positive effects. You can own it by making it a ten-minute part of your daily route. Make it as automatic as brushing your teeth. There are plenty of books, tapes and training programs out there. But as mystical and esoteric as we might make it out to be, the trick isn't learning how to do it – anyone can, there's nothing mystical about it; rather, the trick is staying at it once you know how.

Whether you call it meditation, the relaxation response, or something else entirely (in Christianity, there is the monastic "Jesus Prayer" that is pure meditation), it is a learned skill. It "feels" much like learning to ride a bicycle: until you "get it," as I recall, it wasn't particularly fun. After a couple of spills you might have begun to ask if all this was worth it. But suddenly, one day, *it just happens.* Now it's all yours, and what was all the fuss about?

Keep at it, give yourself the luxury of quietude, and with time, a new sense of awareness and calmness becomes part of you. It will carry over to the stressful times you can't avoid.

From looking inward comes peace and calm. But these important results are simply the tip of an iceberg of benefits. Let me explain.

Many years ago I read about a study of medical students in three Midwestern schools. The researchers wanted to find out what happens to the sense of compassion as students progress through training. The consensus was that, somehow, connectedness with patients diminished as students moved along the road toward becoming doctors.

What was happening here? What were the causes? Poor teaching methods, maybe? Bad choice of candidates to begin with? Some personality quirk that "the system" unconsciously selected for? Did the ever-present malpractice and managed care specter have something to do with it, maybe? It was getting worse as we entered the 1990's, just about the time this study was released.

The researchers followed 236 medical students for as long as eight years. Students were asked to attend regular focus groups, keep diaries about their training experiences and complete periodic personality inventory tests.

They all began medical training for the "right reasons." The vast majority listed "helping others" as their top motivation. By the end of their first year they felt frustrated in that goal, and were saying things like this:

I entered med school as a loving and open and giving person with a goal to help and give to others…by the end of my first year I was sure that medicine was the wrong career choice for me. I was angry that my instructors didn't really seem to care about making physicians, only about making doctors.

Or another:

I feel I have so much to give. I am determined in spite of the way I am taught, that it is right to be involved, empathetic and loving of my patients. In fact, it is the only way I can deal with all the pain inside and around me…

On tests of self-esteem, these students scored about average – *before* they entered medical school. The longer in training, the lower their self-esteem. By the end of the eight-year study nearly a third scored below average, regardless of which personality inventory test was used. And when measured against controls that could be expected to show some of the lowest self esteem, they did even worse: 13% scored lower than patients in an Al-Anon twelve step program; 21% scored lower than hospitalized depressed patients.

Is something wrong with this picture, or what? In teaching lack of involvement with patients to "save" the fledgling doctors' psyches, training programs were squeezing the compassion out of them: *you can't be compassionate and be a doctor* was the message. This was true across the board, whatever the specialty and wherever the student trained.

Efforts to correct this included meditative work in focus groups and training zeroing in on issues between patients and young doctors. The result? A dramatic rise in self-esteem that translated into better doctor-patient relationships.

Again, how we take care of ourselves is a key to how successful we are in relating to others.

This came home to me several years ago when I was working with insurors who provide medical malpractice coverage. I have the "enviable" record of having been sued once, unsuccessfully, in a quarter century of medical practice (yes, being hauled into court just once is *enviable* in our litigious society). I was asked to discuss with other doctors why that might be, in hopes of pinpointing problems and sharing "secrets of success."

Despite memorable news reports of the wrong organ being removed or the wrong patient being cut into, most doctors *are* high on clinical skills and extremely conscientious. It seems sensible to assume that if clinical skills are high quality, lawsuits will be minimal. OK, but it wasn't working that way. Doctors who would rank high on any measure of clinical competence were being sued right and left.

Something I learned very early is that patients expect a doctor to provide treatment on two levels. One is clinical treatment – the diagnosing, prescribing, surgerizing, and the other clinical skills medical training is structured to provide.

At least as important as clinical skills – possibly more so – is personal treatment... very simply, how the practitioner relates to the patient as a person. These were the very skills, remember, that medical students in the study so sorely missed. The bottom line was that otherwise competent doctors were being sued much too often because they couldn't empathize with their patients, didn't understand what their patients were feeling and needed.

Elisabeth Kubler-Ross, one of the pioneers in psychology of death and dying, tells how she learned something very important from an unassuming housekeeper. In the course of researching the awareness of patients near life's end, Kubler-Ross wondered why some patients in the intensive care unit recovered or "lived longer than they should" by most accepted medical criteria.

Searching for what they had in common, she came upon just one thing: the same housekeeper tended their rooms. Kubler-Ross met with this woman. "What do you do when you're in their rooms?" she asked.

No doubt a little intimidated by this well-know physician, the woman said simply, "I clean."

"Do you do *anything* else?" asked Elisabeth gently. "Anything at all?"

"Well, yes," came the halting reply. "I *talk* to them."

She treated them as *people*. Doctors aren't the only healers. This cleaning woman understood healing better than a good many M.D.'s. She understood what people needed, even unconscious or comatose people. Although the cleaning lady's personal psychology wasn't something Kubler-Ross pursued, there is no doubt that this woman also understood herself.

We cannot know, feel or understand others well until we know, feel, and understand ourselves. Stated another way, *once we begin to know who we are, we begin to know who everyone else is.* These aren't static ideas, but dynamic working rules. One leads into the other: knowing ourselves leads us to know others, knowing others leads us to know ourselves.

Patterns such as seeking understanding feed on themselves.

A pattern of giving love fosters a pattern of getting love, just as a pattern of anger invariably produces more anger. The cheerful, smiling, upbeat individual makes you feel good, and earns a cheerful response in return.

If we elect to, we can give rise to a beneficial spiral of personal change and growth that feeds upon itself. More growth means more realization of what *more* we may become, of *who we may become.*

Time magazine's person of the twentieth century was Albert Einstein. Nobody would call him anything less than brilliant, inventive, incisive, creative, perhaps the ultimate independent thinker. He literally reshaped how we see the cosmos and replaced, with his own, the Newtonian laws that were the bedrock of physics. Talk about accomplishment in the span of one lifetime!

Yet, as Mortimer Adler relates in *Six Great Ideas,* Einstein reached the end of his life depressed and even ashamed he had accomplished *so little*. The father of time/space/mass and quantum mechanics realized that *even he* had so much more potential than was ever actualized.

Actualization is one of the fruits of cultivating mindfulness. Is each of us destined to be an Einstein, Mozart or Mother Theresa? They're tough acts to follow, for sure, and the bright-eyed, optimistic answer is we'll never know until we explore ourselves. But at the end of the day, whether we ever come close to fitting one of those great names doesn't matter. After all, those names are already taken.

Each of us, however, can explore and actualize the unique genius that is ours alone. We don't need to be Albert Schweitzer or Bill Gates or Tiger Woods or the pretty Hollywood face *du jour*. We need to be who we *should* be. We need to be who we *can* be. In his or her own unique way, that person is every bit as astounding, fulfilling and necessary as the superstars of our world.

In the backward way that tragedy sometimes dispenses its

lessons, we've seen that happen. Who of us didn't feel proud – and if truth be known, surprised – at how our political leaders acted in the crisis?

Many people seriously questioned whether those at the political helm could meet a critical challenge. But above the din, as one commentator wrote, they were "voices of sanity." Sure, there was the flag-waving posturing and grandstanding, but that's political habit that isn't going to be turned off in an instant. We also, much more essentially, have seen leadership, cooperation, even statesmanship. We've seen our body politic rise to the occasion. Again, a glimpse of *what could be.*

New York City Mayor Rudi Giuliani is one of the most brilliant examples. Until September 11 he was, by conventional wisdom's standards, a political has-been, battered by personal problems and political woes, riding out his closing months in office. Who would have guessed that Giuliani would or *could* be the leader he proved himself? He showed himself to be genuine, an unscripted political figure. Selfless, inspiring, untiring, he has been called "Churchill in a baseball cap" by a *Christian Science Monitor* writer. *That* is actualization.

The stuff our ordinary life, of course, is less heralded, but no less real.

My oldest daughter, Amy, graduated from Medill School of Journalism at Northwestern University. She is a wonderful writer, and soon after graduation she and her talents found their home in a prestigious office on Michigan Avenue in Chicago.

Amy was successful because she was talented, hard-working and dedicated to what she loved – being creative with words on paper. Her work brought financial success, but left her restless... that seems to run in the family.

She began to get involved with Big Sisters on Chicago's South Side, and for three years mentored a young girl from a poor family.

Amy loved the experience so much she made a life-changing decision.

"Dad," this particular phone call began, "I just don't feel like I'm making a difference anymore. I like my job okay, and the pay and benefits are great, but the work isn't what I thought it might be."

My daughter is an anachronism. She is an idealistic, liberal-thinking, self-driven person. She should have come of age during the 1960's. The first thing that ran through my head is *she's packed her bags and is heading off to some third world country!*

"What do you want to do?" I asked tentatively, vowing to stay level-headed about this.

"I want to teach, Dad. Inner city kids."

Every parent who has ever sacrificed to send a child to college, then sees them successful, is very proud. Yet a small piece of me wanted to shout, "Why do you want to throw away your education and good job?"

That moment passed, fortunately. "Go for it, baby," I advised.

Amy worked hard to get her teaching certificate, taking part-time jobs to pay her tuition. Now she's teaching second grade in one of Chicago's toughest inner city schools. She's still scrambling to learn her new job well, but she also knows she is making a difference. She actualized the potential that she came to see as her personal knowledge grew.

To a mighty proud dad, what she is doing is no less heroic than the firemen, policemen, nurses, social workers, and thousands of others who strive to make a difference. They profess what every single person in this world sooner or later realizes. Leo Rosten sums it up well:

The purpose of life is not to be happy. Instead, the purpose of life is to be compassionate, responsible and useful. It is above all to matter, to count and to have made a difference for having lived at all.

I think heaven is like this: a place with no clocks and calendars, an eternal "now" where one has the ability to explore the endless possibilities of self. And I have a feeling it is all rooted in knowing, which is expressed in love and connectedness and giving. It arises from a place where we all, sooner or later, come to know. There, we learn how much alike we all are.

I think that in the aftermath of the tragedies at the World Trade Center and Pentagon and in the Pennsylvania countryside, we may have been afforded a glimpse of heaven.

"My barn has burned to the ground," goes a Taoist saying. "Now I can see the stars."

ACTUALIZATION IS, of course, a two-dollar word for "making it happen." Whether for an individual or organization, successful actualization becomes an almost organic process. When it's working, really working, it's even more than habitual. It becomes as automatic as the dynamics that take place at the cellular level.

The physical healing of a wound, as an example, isn't an event, it's a process. Specialized cells move to the wound's edge. Then they literally change, transforming themselves into a new kind of cell. These new cells – fibroblasts – lay down a protein called collagen that forms the scar.

But the healing process isn't over yet, not by a long shot. The collagen molecule, somewhat like a tiny spring that has been stretched, pulls the edges of the wound together to form the scar we recognize. That the scar becomes less noticeable with time demonstrates that things continue to happen; it's being remodeled and reworked incessantly by the body even years later, all of this in response to the tensions and stresses that affect it.

Like virtually everything else that goes on inside our bodies, all of this happens without us thinking about it. Movement, activity, is constant – it must be for a wound to heal... or for food to be digested, red blood cells oxygenated, waste excreted or skin cells regenerated. We're simply not built as immobile statues of bronze or stone. We are dynamic systems.

This axiom extends beyond the physical. Movement is ideally ongoing, too, in that center of our being that can't be found in the anatomy book. We must, of necessity, move to grow and adapt to change. In doing that, we become complete. We tap into the awesome power for self-discovery and identity that mindfulness offers.

There's a caveat that goes with this optimistic assessment: unlike autonomic bodily processes, mindfulness doesn't happen so neatly and automatically. Here, *movement* means conscious effort. Like meditation, visualizing can be a part of the mindfulness experience – one that fosters movement.

Athletes use visualization all the time: the quarterback or pitcher or golfer will "see" his performance as it unfolds on the playing field of his mind. He *knows* the experience before he's done it. He *owns the truth* of his own potential by being mindful of it. Musicians, actors, singers and other performers have made it one of the tools in their chests, as well.

While most of us earn our living at tasks more mundane than winning on the PGA tour or delivering a boffo Hamlet, many of us also go through the same mental process, probably without being aware of it. Before actually stepping up to the operating table I often would sit and, in my mind, run through each step of the operation ahead. I also would visualize the possible problems and my reactions, as the guide to being *mindful* in the operating theater.

Mindfulness is a key that helps us displace the noise and distraction of our lives. We can be mindful with any task – driving a car, running a race, cooking a meal, being with those we love. After all, being attentive and mindful in the moment we're living is what it's all about – living life fully, getting the most from every minute it offers us.

On one hand, this is all about aloneness, while on the other, it's all about connectedness. Talk of mindfulness sometimes raises an objection that goes something like this: "This aloneness is fine, but I'm not a solitary type. I'm a people person, need others around me, don't do well alone."

Very few of us would choose to be hermits, and mindfulness doesn't ask you to. *Loneliness* and *aloneness* are two very different things.

To be lonely is to lack companionship or attention. It's one of the less desirable realities of the human condition that affects us all at one time or another. I can't support it with statistical proof, but I think loneliness is one of the most insidious epidemics of our time. Our world seems *filled* with lonely people, so many of them cut off from traditional support systems of family, community and place. It seems just as clear that the "hurry sickness" of our culture promotes it, whether we're physically alone or in the middle of a crowd.

Unlike advertisers' promises about using the right toothpaste or wearing the right sneakers, listening to your internal wisdom doesn't guarantee a first place finish in life's popularity contests. There are always times in life when doing the right thing threatens to distance you from others; that's when we have to do the heavy lifting of weighing priorities. My stand on patient-centered healthcare has at times isolated me from people in my profession.

Doctors and health system managers with a with a stake in the *status quo* see me as a "disturbing element." I've been told bluntly that my views are outside those held by the club of peers, and these peers damn well wish I wouldn't stir the pot – *we have enough problems already, thank you very much*, and besides, there isn't time to do all the things I advocate.

It will always be a curiosity to me, if not a mystery, that doctors react so negatively to an effort aimed at regaining the very thing they entered healthcare for. I wish you could know the times I have felt the loneliness of rejection when this occurs.

Loneliness happens. Aloneness doesn't, unless you make it. Moreover, aloneness fosters exactly the opposite feelings. Those who are alone and comfortable with that aloneness are filled with power and a serenity. It's as if you're meeting your best friend in a place that promotes peace and calm. And in a sense, that's just what happens when you allow yourself an internal place of constant acceptance and love.

We need the calm of aloneness to gain focus. This is another of those lessons we inherently *know, but*.... Imagine you're in a rowboat on a turbulent sea, in sight of land but still in danger of being swamped. Your goal, obviously, is to row your boat to shore. Wind and water buffet the boat and it's all you can do to keep bailing and stay afloat. How much effort can you devote to rowing to safety? Your only hope is that the storm subsides before you wear out!

We need to give ourselves the luxury of sitting quietly in an empty mental room, or to extend the boat metaphor, on placid water. I encourage you to stop, be quiet with yourself, and trust that it will lead you into a sea that is warm and calm, unaffected by the elements above. Then, when you choose to leave the stillness, you'll find your waiting tasks can be better understood and accomplished.

The archer, in that moment before he releases the arrow, does two things. He pulls the string and arrow back, in the *opposite direction* of his goal. This gives the arrow the energy to reach its target. Then, at the perfect moment just before release, he pauses. He stops for that instant to correct his aim.

Mindfulness is like this. There will always be a new shore to reach or target to hit. It is the personal preparation we do *before* getting into the boat or fixing the arrow onto the bowstring that equips one for success.

ANYONE WHO LIVES the life of perpetually juggling demands

and responsibilities is no doubt wondering where to find time for mindfulness when just keeping up is a chore. The world, it's easy to assume, won't wait for our delay. We expect it will march us by.

Experience proves otherwise. *Those who choose to be mindful reset the timer*. They march to *their* timetable, not the world's. It's amazing to see how often the world adapts to *them* as a result.

Joseph Cardinal Bernadine, former archbishop of the Diocese of Chicago, wrote a book near the end of his life entitled *The Gift of Peace*. In it, he chronicled the closing days of his personal journey. You might expect that someone who had spent nearly fifty years as a cleric, much of that as a senior spiritual leader, would know all about peace and serenity.

No, we're all pilgrims. Only after he found he was dying from pancreatic cancer, and learned to put aside so many of his seemingly critical duties, did he realize where peace comes from. "The gift of peace, in all its glory and Godlike majesty," he writes, "comes not from holding on, but instead, from *letting go*."

Letting go. It sounds so risky, and always has. Nearly 2,500 years ago, an Indian prince named Siddhartha confronted that same concern. His conclusion was as straightforward as it was insightful. And it was remarkably like advice a counselor, steeped in the psychology and science of our age, might dispense.

"Let go, but don't do it on my say-so or anyone else's," said Siddhartha, who came to be known as the Buddha. "Prove it to yourself. Find one thing that you can't let go of, and then do." Just let it go. Forget controlling and micromanaging and impossible standards and all the rules about "how it has to be done."

Let go, and as you do, listen to yourself. Open your heart to *you* and to the possibilities you hold. Open yourself to the answers you hold, in the place you will find them. Quietude allows it to happen.

When you have let go, and your hands are free, you just might grab onto what you've always been seeking: the wisdom within.

Here are some summary thoughts:

1. Don't allow yourself to get stuck trying to answer the unanswerable. *Why* can be a trap that keeps you from moving ahead.

2. Grasp the lessons that bad times offer. They can be life-enhancing and even life-changing.

3. Realize you can't change the world. Start with yourself: we can change how we, individually, respond to the world.

4. Give yourself time for mindfulness. Be alone with yourself. One of the most important gifts you can offer yourself is the opportunity to know yourself.

5. Rather than seeking to rebuild what was, use tragedy's lessons as a blueprint to build what can be.

"Learn to get in touch with the silence within yourself," wrote Elisabeth Kubler-Ross, "and know that everything in this life has a purpose.

3

The Power of Connection

I was at Liberty State Park in New Jersey early on September 12, part of a medical response team. The walking wounded from the World Trade Center were being funneled here.

I had driven past Liberty Park, across the Hudson River from the southern tongue of Manhattan, hundreds of times before on my way into the city. Now it was unfamiliar and surreal. Beyond the river, dense smoke seemed to rise from the very earth, filling the sky where the Towers stood just hours before. Fires flickered.

Many of us on the other side might have thought we were seeing Hell, a medieval hell of sulfurous fumes and flames of the kind Dante envisioned. The breeze, always fickle on the river, zigzagged, sometimes sending smoke westward toward the park. Ash floated down in a gentle drizzle. The smell of smoke and ozone was everywhere, on clothing and in the air.

People milled around Liberty Island looking for loved ones. Some held pictures, and others, signs with names. The scene was like that grainy footage of war-torn Europe that we see on the History Channel. All about me, "unbelievable" was on everyone's lips.

Inside the makeshift aid station, a pall hung over the medical workers who had responded to early and urgent calls for help. At the first shock, when massive casualties seemed inevitable, anxious appeals had gone out to surrounding states for nurses, EMT's and doctors. Who could have imagined these would be unneeded, that even massive casualties would prove to be too optimistic a notion? The enormity of death was beginning to reveal itself.

At St. Vincent's Hospital, where the most seriously inured from Ground Zero would be taken, staff was "standing by," the radio reported. So were medics at makeshift aid stations not far from the epicenter. Although the radio and TV reporters mostly had the good grace not to say it yet, the chance of finding survivors was dropping geometrically. In any disaster, the first twenty-four hours are the "golden hours" for recovering victims alive. Rather than the antici-pated hundreds or thousands being pulled from the rubble, the res-cued were being counted by ones. Screams would have been terri-ble, but less so than the silence.

Ferries, mechanically crossing to and from lower Manhattan, unloaded somber hordes of ghost people covered with ashy film. With every new wave of arrivals, people crowded in and strained to hear any news of survivors. Medics looked for the injured, no mat-ter how minor, seeking to do something to help. Both news and ways to help were limited. Some of the arrivals said little. Many stared and spoke distantly, as if channeling a voice not their own. Others, as people in emotional shock sometimes do, babbled.

I noticed a striking sameness, though, to their words. They were talking not about themselves, but others... about heroic deeds and those who stopped to help at their own peril; about the firefighters, who would be buried in the rubble, charging in as the office workers streamed out; about friends and coworkers who they feared lost.

On those rare occasions they did mention themselves, it was about how they had been helped, or how they had tried to help oth-ers. None spoke boastfully, no one criticized. It struck me they could have been impartial observers, reporting in a detached way about something extraordinary they had just witnessed.

They weren't thinking about Number One. It was as if ego, itself, had been a casualty of the deadly explosions.

Never had I seen anything like this, where nothing mattered but one's fellow man. The catastrophe in its enormity had transformed as disparate a group of people as you could imagine into a population of compassionate and giving human beings. "Feeling good" was something few here could claim, but in a way that touched the very soul, it felt good to be here.

An Hispanic man cried as he told how a fireman had literally sheltered him with his body as debris rained from collapsing Tower One. Then, like some pied piper in a terrible story, the fireman began shouting for people to follow him, linking into a human chain. They ran through what he called "midnight," the blinding, acrid cloud of smoke and debris, seeking any refuge from the certain death of airborne girders and concrete. In the malestrom they became separated. Several blocks further on, the man found himself being pulled into a restaurant that would be his sanctuary.

In a few hours he made his way back to the Trade Center, looking to help. There he learned that those he had fled with and the fireman were lost and presumed dead. His tears cut rivulets into the chalk-white dust on his face.

Why do we extend ourselves so readily in a time of great peril or need? Adrenaline? Simply because others truly need our help? Do we pass some internal threshold, maybe, and decide the situation is *serious enough* to merit help? Is it we don't worry about being rebuffed in a crisis? Or is it that in our mundane, workaday world, we're too jaded or occupied to care?

A psychologist versed in crowd behavior could no doubt explain it all in detail. Being too jaded or occupied is, however, part of it. A week after the attack, a psychiatric social worker in New York City explained how "different" things had become: "The street people have never eaten so well," she explained. "People used to walk on by, they wanted to make street people invisible. Now, they stop and give them money, even take the time to get them a meal. I've even heard of pedestrians going up to street people and asking what they can do to help them!"

Are people changed by tragedy? Some surely are. In the aftermath of the kamikaze attacks, we saw evil met with 100,000 acts of kindness. In the month after the attacks, by some estimates, charities collected as much as a billion dollars to help victims and their families. There is surely some cosmic law that humanity's worst draws forth humanity's best. "Prosperity doth best discover vice," wrote Sir Francis Bacon, "but adversity doth best discover virtue."

Perhaps this force keeps evil from perpetually gaining the upper hand. A week after the destruction, a *New York Times* article tried explaining it by saying that the change was evolutionary, Darwinian even. One radio commentator had scoffed at such a thought, but I'm not so sure the *Times* piece was far off base. I believe that we are hard-wired for such compassion. Within each of us is a spark that I believe is divine, a piece of unbounded goodness that can take over and guide our response.

I know I witnessed any number of things that confirm what I have always wanted to trust: that human beings are basically damn good... that selflessness is a response that brings us to the brink of God's threshold... that love is, in the end, the ultimate and maybe only worthwhile reaction.

I couldn't help but compare the social worker's experience with something I had once seen in a hospital surgeons' lounge. In a corner of a bulletin board, in the handwritten scrawl only a doctor could produce, was this quip: *Life would be perfect if it weren't for other people!*

I suspected the anonymous author really meant patients. Admittedly, I'm no mind reader. Maybe he meant other doctors, or perhaps other OR staff. Maybe the writer just thought it was "cute," and didn't even think much beyond that. Whatever the quip was supposed to mean, it forced me to pause at its cynicism.

I wonder if the poster has ever been on the receiving end – a patient? I'm convinced that should be a medical school require-ment: every fledgling doctor ought to have a "procedure" done, whether he needs it or not.

Interns training to be family practitioners at Long Beach Memorial Hospital in Southern California have a rare and wonder-ful opportunity to do just that.

Before they start the program, they can be admitted to the hos-pital under assumed names with fictitious diagnoses. They spend three days as patients, IV inserted, eating hospital food, having blood drawn, getting sponge baths, enduring the battery of diagnos-tic tests, the enforced regimen, the five channels on the rented TV, waking up every couple of hours to have vitals taken, and maybe even experiencing the proverbial roommate from hell.

These fortunate young healers-in-training learn very quickly that life is much different on the other side of the bedpan. They come to understand that what's routine for the person in the white coat is probably anything but for the one in the hospital gown. Having experienced, they can begin to understand. You can bet that these doctors are going to be much more connected, empathetic and compassionate physicians.

That also helps explain why the street people enjoyed such unex-pected bounty. Those passersby can understand *how it is...* they can begin comprehend misfortune and what it's truly about. As a nation we had been largely isolated from that during the go-go years of high-flying stocks, a boom economy and a day-trading millionaire on every other corner. It had even become fashionable to assume that those who didn't make it were made of lesser moral stuff.

We really *are* the products of our experience, which has been pretty darned good for a long while. We might not have *everything* we want, but we're not doing too shabby. We certainly have everything we *need,* and generally have the resources to pamper and indulge ourselves and our families. We boast a prosperity such as history has never seen.

I read recently that between thirty-six and thirty-seven million people, a fifth of them children, go hungry in this richest nation in the world. I don't know if that's a good number or not – statistical sleight of hand is commonplace enough that any shocking statistic gets a jaundiced look. Let's say for argument's sake that "just" thirty million people are hungry, or "just" twenty million. Or "just" two million. It's too many. What must it be like for a parent to hear a child cry because she is hungry? How will malnutrition affect that child physically, developmentally? Actually, we do know, all too well, what it does to developing bodies and minds.

When our parents cajoled us to "eat your food, there are starving people in the world," maybe they *were* using guilt tactics to get us to eat broccoli. They also were telling us something else, although it most probably was lost on kids facing a mountain of detested vegetables. Chances are that during the War, or even in the darkest days of the Depression, they had seen hunger firsthand.

Do we *really understand* hunger? Walk down any street, or even stand in front of a mirror, and dote on the human midsection. Question answered, right?

Few of us, thankfully, will ever experience life without a roof overhead, without the comfort of family and friends, without the security of knowing that tomorrow, like today, we will have what we need. What must it be like, day after day, to depend on others' generosity for the very things of survival?

Tragedy is a teacher. Now, suddenly, when so many people are hurting and our security blanket has been pulled from around us, we can begin to comprehend. Misfortune can hit you when you're walking down the street or sitting at your desk, and there's sometimes not a damn thing you can do about it.

In a very real sense, the man on the street has "been there," if not actually, then in real-time images of suffering. Like the young doctors masquerading as patients in California, those passersby in Manhattan, and a lot of other places, have become much more connected, empathetic and compassionate.

DR. GREG RYS, friend and psychologist, works in Somerset County, Pennsylvania. It's a rural area, not a place that makes the news often or gets many outside visitors. But it did both on September 11.

There, just outside the small town of Shanksville, United Airlines Flight 93 nose-dived into a reclaimed strip mine, killing the 44 people aboard. As we now know, the heroism of the passengers probably kept Flight 93 from reaching a Washington or Camp David target.

Greg, who works with cancer and heart disease patients at nearby Windber Medical Center, was a caregiver to others who had assembled at the crash site to begin the grisly task of gathering remains and investigating the accident.

These people come across as a stoic, even tough bunch: State Troopers, FBI investigators, forensic anthropologists, morticians, Red Cross and Salvation Army workers, and local firefighters and paramedics. They've done things like this before, most of them. But no matter how many times you've done this, you hardly get used to it; they're not nearly as tough as they let on. Like guards that need to be guarded, these caregivers need to be cared for.

"I provided mostly schmooze therapy at the crash site and morgue," says Greg. Schmooze therapy, he explained, "is the sophisticated clinical term for walking around and talking. I did a lot of shaking hands, thanking them, listening, letting them know that what they're doing is important. We all need that, even *tough* reach out and serve others. It refuels us, it heals us, and makes us want to shake off our distress and begin again."

Greg recalled how some at the scene tried to joke and pretend it's just a job, and others seemed to be embarrassed by the seeming inconsequence of their duties.

"But their eyes belied their caring and the human need to be recognized. We knew how much we cared. We were just afraid or embarrassed to admit it."

That's something we'll be contending with years from now – pain that people helping now will feel only then. Many who do this grim work find that their feelings and emotions come to the surface only years later. After all, cops and crash scene investigators and morgue workers aren't the kind who are supposed to cry, or even hurt. They're the ones who have to stay in control.

But no matter how we try to put it off, we have to come to grips with mourning before we move on. Most of us will move on in time and be fine. Others, especially those for whom the experience was close and the pain personal, will find they can deal with it only later, and sometimes, much later.

The events of September 11 produced many heroes, but Greg noticed a curious reaction when workers at the crash site were called "heroes." They would protest, some even vigorously. Part of that is no doubt our discomfort with effusive praise; another part of it, perhaps, is their desire not to detract from the even greater heroism of others. There were martyrs on that flight, but they weren't the terrorists who saw the death of innocents as instant tickets to heaven.

Greg thinks there's something more to the discomfort he saw. He remembers years ago working with Vietnam vets. They also would be embarrassed or even angry at being called heroic – despite many remarkable acts that certainly were heroic by most definitions. "I recalled their lesson," said Greg. "They would say, 'we're not heroes, we were just fellow human beings caring for each other.'

"To their minds, 'heroes' made them sound like gods. They understood that all the acts of caring, all the selfless acts of bravery, love and sacrifice, are ultimately *very* human. Maybe these things are *us as humans* when we're at our best. Maybe the essence of our nature as humans," says Greg, "is to be loving, self-sacrificing and charitable."

IN TIMES OF NEED we are assured by countless little healing acts of mercy and kindness. We both need them and want them. Most of us would prefer the quick fix of a miracle, but you know, miracles could be dangerous things. If miracles abounded each time we were in trouble, could be ordered up like a pay-per-view movie, we would become essentially useless. Would our purpose for living be nothing more than to enjoy a lifelong, cosmic Club Med? Hedonism in measured doses has its appeal, but as a steady diet, most of us would find it very unsatisfying.

As I see it, we would not only become essentially useless, but life would become meaningless. At best, we would be reduced to the level of lower animals, whose highest purpose is to create another generation guided by the same, unflinching instinctive knowledge. At worst, we would soon become totally redundant. In a miracle-laden world, would we ever make the effort to understand anything beyond sensory experience? Would we – *could we* – reach out to others as each person in his own little world snaps fingers to have needs satisfied and sorrows erased? There would be no need for me lend a hand to you in your strife… miracles-on-demand would make that redundant.

Most of us now know that such miracles don't routinely happen. What does happen is the human touch of mercy and caring. And perhaps that is miracle enough.

God is a really funny guy, I've learned. When things seem their bleakest he delivers punch lines that help us heal.

One such experience came to me at a time when I needed it most. My youngest daughter, Susan, had just died. I mourned for a life too short and tried, as I always did, to cover my grief with work. There was no reason to laugh, even if I could have.

I was standing in a surgery holding area, reassuring a mom that her child's hernia repair would go well and quickly. I happened to hear two little boys chatting like magpies. They were no more than four or five, sitting up in their litters and waiting to be wheeled into the OR.

I found out later that child number one was to have a tonsillectomy and adenoidectomy. His mother had also signed him up for a circumcision, no doubt wanting to avoid a second round of surgery and anesthesia. This boy had no clue was a "circ" was, and his mother no doubt thought it would be easier to explain in retrospect. Boy number two was to have the identical operations, *sans* circ.

A little while later, my surgery complete, I exited from the OR to see the nurses laughing hysterically. Then they explained:

As boy number two was being readied to go into surgery, he again found himself beside his friend, who had just been wheeled out. He was groggy but awake. Boy number two asked how it was; his friend spend a few seconds taking stock. He swallowed a few times uncomfortably, and then lifted the sheet and saw the dressing from his circumcision. His eyes grew wide. "My throat hurts," he said hoarsely, "but wait 'til you find out where your adenoids are!"

We all get blindsided sometimes and surprised by where "our adenoids" reside. We're always blindsided by tragedy. In our pain, we lose sight of the power of love, concern and good humor. In our pain, others reveal them to us, and help us understand that even this terrible time will pass.

When I heard the story of the adenoids, I laughed, the first time in a long while. I often have wondered if the story was true, or if the nurses had concocted it for my benefit.

COULD THERE BE a greater hell than a Nazi death camp? Any thinking person is sickened to think of humans rounded up for the flimsiest of excuses, packed into cattle cars, then slaughtered and disposed of with industrial efficiency.

Eight million concentration camp deaths and the perspective of more than a half century still won't allow us to understand. *As if we could.* Our species may see the day when the brain can explain itself, and even fathom the very mysteries of creation, but I believe the human mind will be no closer to understanding consummate evil.

Evil, though, never manages to win over the human spirit. Viktor Frankl shows that unforgettably in *Man's Search for Meaning,* a book drawn from his experience as concentration camp prisoner. It is one of the last century's most moving testaments to the indomitable human spirit.

Frankl speaks of six men who quietly stood out in the hell of Auschwitz. In a Kafkaesque world of insanity, precisely designed to strip away every shred of humanity, these prisoners held onto inner peace, strength, dignity and purpose.

Each morning the six would put aside some of their meager daily ration of bread scraps and a few ounces of watery potato soup. They did this realizing well that even the "full ration" was inadequate to sustain life. Death by starvation was part of the ghastly efficiency of the Nazi killing machine.

Each evening, when they returned from their forced labor, they sought out the weakest in the barracks. They gave them the saved food. This gift was life itself in a place where strength to work was the one chance of fending off the gas chamber for one more day.

These men, Frankl relates, did more. They would comfort those whose health, strength and spirit were shattered. In the freezing barracks, offering the skimpiest protection from the icy Polish winter, these men would take the sickest to their bunks, giving their dying fellow humans warmth and comfort. When death came, its chosen ones were surrounded by the peace of loving human warmth.

When the liberators reached Auschwitz, black smoke still drifting from the crematoria chimneys, only a handful of prisoners were able to get to their feet to greet them. Among those who could were the six, the ones who gave when every rational thought would have urged the opposite. In their giving, they were nourished and sustained.

"To live is to suffer," Frankl writes. "To survive is to find meaning in the suffering." There's no *why*. There *is* meaning in suffering, profound meaning that can lead us to wisdom.

Part of the wisdom is a simple but immutable law: *by giving we get.*

SOME YEARS AGO I received a call from a woman in Montoursville, a one-light town in northeastern Pennsylvania. Montoursville is one of the dwindling number of places that time seems to have missed. Change the cars along the street and the plastic letters spelling out this week's movie, and a photo from today could easily pass for early twentieth century.

Montoursville also was rocked by a tragedy. It was home to seventeen high school children and their adult chaperons who left one summer day for a school-sponsored trip to France. Their flight, TWA flight 800, exploded and crashed into the Atlantic. All aboard were killed.

The phone call came from a very sweet woman I had met when I spoke at a nurses' conference some time before. She asked if I would come to Montoursville and help the community heal from this horrible tragedy. Her daughter was one of the victims.

I went there, and spoke with clergy, families, community leaders, and children in several venues, hearing about how much this community needed to heal. What I learned, among many other things, was more than I ever gave to them.

I learned that besides families and schools, communities raise children (Hillary R. Clinton called it a *village*). I saw in Montoursville that a community teaches its younger members how to prepare for life, even as they cope with the death of brothers, sisters, cousins and friends. Even though this was a closely-knit small town, in a way that only small towns seem able, the people had never been more closely knit than in the face of this terrible loss. They asked me to help them heal. They were hurting, as anyone surely would, but they already had healed.

Who you are isn't just what your family teaches you, but also what you learn from the other people around you. The people in Montoursville reminded me of that. They were fortunate in having retained the sense of village that our modern culture has largely obliterated. Their community helped raise healers of the future as they grieved for their own losses. They knew intuitively who to lean on. Relationships were forged and strengthened. They supported and consoled one another. The community was connected.

A few years later I was in Littleton, Colorado, a place name forever linked with the Colombine High School tragedy. Here, I listened to the grieving of people whose experience was very different. Littleton was perhaps the prototype upscale American suburb as the twentieth century ended. In many ways, as often-transient bedroom communities tend to be, it was a distant community.

I heard the story, for example, of the neighbor who heard smashing glass. The sound came from a nearby garage, the Saturday before the massacre, and it went on for perhaps five full minutes. Obviously something wasn't right, but the neighbor who heard all this continued washing his car, preferring not to get involved.

It came out later that the kids who would carry out the murderous rampage at Colombine were making glass shrapnel for the bomb they hoped to detonate in the school.

Did Columbine "make" the young killers who caused so much pain to families and the community? That would be an unfair and certainly hurtful judgment, as well as a very simplistic one. Yet you can't help but wonder what might have happened had someone just taken the time to investigate the shattering glass... how a simple act of caring and connectedness might have made all the difference.

WE'RE BUILT AS social animals. Unlike newly-hatched turtles or tadpoles, born with instinctive knowledge of how to be what they are, young humans require decades of nurturing and teaching from other humans. While this might seem that nature is being inefficient, it's one of our great advantages: humans have the capacity to change, and quickly, through modifying our learned culture. Alone among living things in this respect, we aren't hobbled by a need to rely on evolutionary mutation stretching over millennia. We have choice, and that, philosophers and theologians have long maintained, is what makes us human.

From the most down-and-out street person to the wealthiest and most pampered debutante, we depend on other people for our well-being. Others keep our transportation functioning, our bellies full, our children looked after, our homes repaired, our public spaces livable. They keep our ailments treated, teeth repaired, hair cut, engines tuned, food processed, minds engaged, hearts filled... the list stretches on. That's life in an interconnected society. It serves us well.

Yet ironically, as we become increasingly interconnected, we are becoming less connected. Let me explain.

Abraham Maslow's "hierarchy of needs," familiar to generations of introduction to psychology graduates, speaks of the basic requirements of food, shelter and relationship. Around these essential needs clusters a universe of wants.

We *could* subsist in a cave if we had to – that's shelter – but we don't want *just* shelter, of course. Neither do we want *just* clothing, or *just* cars, or *just* food. We're livin' large, far beyond a life of subsisting on roots we've dug and game we've bagged. That's an obvious benefit of the interaction and specialization we call civilization.

Maslow's hierarchy makes it all look simple. It isn't, not at all. Needs have a peculiar way of becoming wants... which have a pesky habit of turning into needs. Moreover, *need-wants* are both self-perpetuating and constantly accelerating. Some three thousand years ago the Hindus saw this. As they're wont to do, they left an insightful observation: "To try to extinguish the desire for riches with more riches is like trying to extinguish a fire with oil."

Can we have it all? *Ever?* Certainly not, we know that. Yet we *act like* we can. If that were simply a harmless diversion – some benign adult version of make-believe – we could shrug and say, "If that makes you happy, have a ball!"

One of the realities, however, is we're just not good enough to have it all or do it all. When pursuit of the unobtainable is at our center stage, something has to give. *What* gives is predictable: invariably, the third need Maslow speaks of: *relationships.* (Did you notice how easily we had scooted right by them?) Relationships, it seems to me, have been the sacrificial victim of need-wants.

We've become so adept at the game it's easy to tell ourselves relationships really are *optional.* They're *not.* They're a *need,* just like Maslow says. There's a huge difference between wants and needs. Wants are self-gratifying. Needs speak of the essential.

Relationships are vital to wellness, another of those "soft ideas" backed by hard science. A baby needs human contact for proper development – infants shortchanged on human touch become a Pandora's box of developmental problems. Studies of ICU nurseries show that premature babies who are not held and touched for a generous portion of their day die more frequently, stay on ventilators longer, are in the hospital longer, and are slower to gain weight.

This is not some infantile need we grow out of, either. People who live alone – or more specifically, people who have little or no social contact – live on average seven years less than people in supportive relationships. Drs. Mary and Wayne Sotile of the Department of Psychology at Wake Forest University have done landmark work in this field. Working with patients in intensive care cardiac units, they have discovered something that was obvious, yet obviously underestimated.

If a person has had one heart attack, what psychological factors put him at risk for another? That's the question they wanted to answer. We all know the link between heart disease and stress, high cholesterol, morbid obesity, smoking, high blood pressure and diabetes. The Sotiles discovered that as critical as all those factors are, they're still not as risky as going it alone. If you had one deeply personal, intimate relationship that you had taken time to nurture, whether that be a spouse, child, parent or even a very close friend, you could cut your risk of a second heart attack in half! This is powerful medicine.

It is very heartening – no pun intended – that a physician of such high repute as Dean Ornish, who helped us get heart healthy with vigorous attention to diet, exercise and meditation, has written a book called *Love and Survival.* How very fascinating that such a wonderful clinician and scientist would write about the healing power of love and relationship.

Yes, medical science has been slow in taking that message to heart, and yes, there there's still a constitutional wariness of science that can't be dispensed via a pill or scalpel. But how far we've come! When I graduated form medical school in the 1970's, linking lack of love and heart attacks would have made the "established medical community" laugh 'til its sides hurt. The clown who suggested it would have been the object of an occupational stoning.

I have witnessed dozens of patients who simply have given up life, in spite of having the physical stuff to live and grow. They had "nothing to live for." Their self-inflicted mercy killings speak to their soul-deadening absence of family, friends, lovers – or worse, the void in knowledge and experience of themselves.

I had an experience that brought home very personally how lacking we've become in the relationship department. Remember a few pages ago when I suggested every doctor ought to have a "procedure" himself? I had one, although it actually came closer to killing me than I like.

It began, as these things always do, in a most ordinary way. I was scheduled to deliver an after dinner talk to a group in Philadelphia. Nursing a cold for weeks, I was in less than top form to start with. I picked my way through dinner – unusual. As the product of an Italian family where mealtime was the sun our universe revolved around, I can usually tear through a good meal like a combine through a Kansas grain field. This night, I felt weak and dizzy as I stood up. You might say my evening went steadily down from there.

I became very short of breath, like the wind had been knocked out of me. After a few steps I collapsed in a heap near the podium. Normally, you would expect an audience to rise *en masse* and run to my aid, right? *Wrong.*

Some in the audience, you see, knew me and my penchant for resorting to the outrageous to make a point. "Leo's at it again," they no doubt figured, assuming my collapse was a carefully-staged part of the show. They can't be faulted. How many speakers have you ever seen collapse, *bam!*, right on the stage in front of you? But it was no put-up job. I couldn't get air.

Finally – it was certainly a matter of seconds, although it seemed agonizing minutes to me – a cardiologist in the front row noticed my skin taking on a peculiar gray-blue tinge. He ran up onto the stage and announced what seemed obvious for a keeled-over middle-aged guy who ate a lot of banquet meals: "This man is having a heart attack!" I was more than glad for his intervention, but my self-inventory didn't seem to be revealing heart attack symptoms. Gasping for air, there was no way to tell him that I had no pain other than the agony of panic, and was "just" extremely short of breath.

A friend in the audience drove me to the ER at a good hospital, two blocks away. I insisted that he drop me off, it would be easier and quicker than finding a parking space in Philadelphia. Now the adventure really began. Since I walked to the check-in desk under my own power rather than being rolled in by paramedics, it was "obvious" I wasn't too serious. Commanding the desk was a clerk who was sending out a definite message: "Don't bother trying, I've seen it all." I did the best mime I could, trying to tell her I needed to be seen.

"I can't breathe," I mouthed, clutching my throat. She wasn't going to be impressed. "We're busy, you'll have to wait your turn," she announced in an implicit rebuke of my bad manners. "Please take a seat." She announced the conversation's end by lowering her head, returning to her word processor screen, and shooting an arm toward the waiting area.

Huh? Stunned, hardly in any condition to argue, and even a bit ashamed at being scolded, I did as I was told. The patient in the chair next to me saw quickly that something was seriously wrong. "Something is *really wrong* with that guy," I could see her telling the admissions clerk. Suddenly, a nurse saw me and sprinted for a wheelchair.

I was whisked into an emergency room cubicle, the cardiac "crash cart" rumbling after me, as doctors seemed to sprout up like mushrooms after rain. In their flurry, they didn't notice me doing my damnedest to tell them something. *No, I'm not having a heart attack, I can't catch my breath, something else is going on.* Since this whole bizarre episode began, nobody recognized that I had something to add to this surreal conversation. All about me, it never included me. "We're in charge," they seemed to be saying, "shut up and stay out of the way."

When we focus on the problem, we seem to absolve ourselves from the need to focus on the people. Why do we allow this disconnect?

There was a great example of that in Robin Williams' movie portrayal of Dr. Patch Adams. Those who saw it might remember the woman on the litter, obviously ill, surrounded by a crowd of doctors. Residents were making reports to "the attending" – the head honcho, spouting off test results and vitals. In the midst of all this talking about the patient in front of her face, Dr. Adams drops the bombshell question: "What's her name?"

The stares go back and forth as the medical crowd realizes that, gol-eeee, nobody has the foggiest. They know her electrolytes, cardiogram, white cell count, and an entire host of test results and physical findings, but not her name. In the course of treating this woman's illness, she had in fact, become her disease. The focus had become so narrow, so restricted, that she no longer had any identity for these doctors beyond her pathology.

Dehumanized is the word for it, and we allow doctors and other authority figures to get away with it. As my hospital experience showed me, there's sometimes little defense.

After what seemed like an eternity, a nurse – God bless nurses – said the words I longed to hear: "Maybe he can't catch his breath." *Bingo!* As best I could, I tried to nod in eager agreement, although I'm sure nobody noticed. They whisked me away to radiology for a chest x-ray and CAT scan.

A few minutes later, there it was, glowing on the film like an aura around a saint's head: a large abscess of my right pleural cavity, the result of a neglected pneumonia. *Pneumonia?* I thought the runny nose and cough of the last two weeks were just a lingering case of flu topped off with jet lag. You know what they say about one who's his own physician having a fool for a patient.

Within fifteen minutes I had a 12-gauge needle and catheter in my right chest draining off fluid, more than a quart. I could breathe!

I was remanded to the intensive care unit and connected to their impressive array of machinery and wires. I noticed something right away about the "great doctor" they assigned me – he *was* great, I knew, because he told me. My ICU room was barely the size of a closet – two steps would have brought him from doorway to my bedside – but he hardly ever came in.

Curious, I thought, how he would talk from the doorway, usually with his hand on the knob. It was as if he were just sticking his head in on the way to somewhere else. Except with a stethoscope, he never touched me. Maybe he thought that since I was a surgeon, I was a "big boy," and didn't need a consoling pat, comforting touch, or even a handshake. He certainly did a fine job of stripping it to the clinical essentials; I wouldn't be surprised if HMO managers had a picture of him on their desks.

On the third hospital day I still had a high fever and cough. I felt plain rotten. X-rays showed fluid building up again. "You need to have a chest surgeon involved in your care," the doctor said. I mumbled some terse agreement. I was still in no position to argue, and this Type A in a white coat hardly brought out the conversationalist in me. "By the way," he added as his parting shot, "do you know who Jim Henson was?"

"Yes," I replied, "the Muppet guy."

"He died of what you have," said my doctor. He gazed off, as if pondering his profound words, then turned and left.

My first thought – actually, my second, the first was what an incredible ass this man was – was how that would play to a patient with no experience in what was going on. It wasn't playing all that great to *me*, and I *did* know something about it. "Jim Henson was rich and famous," a *normal* patient probably would have reasoned. "He could have had any doctor he wanted, any hospital, the best treatment in the world, and probably did... for the same thing I have. And Jim Hanson's *dead!*" How's he going to judge *his* chances, and how might that affect his healing?

Chest surgery was followed by thirteen more days recovering. I even saw my surgeon three times in those two weeks, as well as his partners and physician's assistant and nurse and medical student and resident. For the life of me, I cannot remember any of their names.

I *can* tell you who helped me heal during my hospital stay, whose names I do remember. Three people: the day nurse, the evening nurse and the night nurse. Each shift, each would spend a few minutes with me. Maybe they would sit at my beside, touch my shoulder or hand, ask about my family. They treated me like a person rather than a disease. Doctors should have learned a long time ago what nurses know about relationships.

So many of our roadblocks to relating with others come from behavior we call Type A. The *A*, incidentally, stands for *arrogant*. To some extent, Type A coping tendencies are a "natural response." Most of us develop these tendencies, according to psychologist Dr. Wayne Sotile. We nurture those ego-centered mannerisms, and when stressed, strike out with our attempts to control the situation for ourselves. While these mannerisms may give the illusion of helping to manage our "big lives," they ultimately hurt our relationships.

Each of us has our own Type A examples, probably by the dozens. We've all come face-to-face with the insufferable salesperson who's more committed to putting down the customer than to making the sale. Or the hoity-toity waitperson bent upon exposing the diner as a culinary oaf. Or the public servant who handles building permits, tax collection or parking tickets, whose goal seems to be to infuse the world with ill will. The best thing about those relationships is they're fleeting.

Being in any kind of ongoing relationship with others, whether across the dinner table or across the conference table, is mostly an ongoing endeavor. It takes conscious effort to do it right, because our natural tendency is to treat others as being there for us. Our habit is to always make it about *me*. We judge this person or that event by how it affects me and my goals, what it has to do with my direction in life. Only occasionally do we stop to really consider the autonomy and individuality of others, and how we're affecting them.

It's easy to see what Type A behavior does where human interactions are concerned. It automatically distances us from the people we most need to hear. When the Type A tendencies are in the driver's seat, there's always an abundance of unnecessary control – not only is the Type A accustomed to taking control, but he *knows* he *should* be in control. What the Type A is really doing is discounting the competency of others. Control becomes the obvious response to a real internal need, and the Type A becomes obsessively competitive to win it. He has the better answer, can do it best, needs to win to show who's the "better person."

Have you ever, in a hurry to get somewhere, pushed an elevator button that's already illuminated? I've done it, and we've seen it a thousand times. That's classic Type A, "center of the universe" syndrome. Better yet, we've all seen that annoying, annuity-for-cardiologists-type who hits the button not once, but repeatedly. He stands there, tapping away as furiously as a telegrapher sending out an SOS. And he is, of course, sending out a distress call. He won't make the elevator move faster, but, oh, how he wishes he could. He's crying out for – actually, acting out – the control he can't have.

It only widens the gaps between others and ourselves. If the Type A acts out often enough, he drifts into a virtual exhaustion similar to burnout. This happens everywhere, in husband-wife relationships, in relationships at work or even with friends. The receiver, facing a kind of burnout all his own, learns quickly to keep his distance. The other thing the *A* stands for is advice to the wise: *avoid him.* Unless, of course, the one on the receiving end is also a Type A, which means we're going to see *action*.

It's a wonder we have any friends or family left who talk to us.

And the sad thing is, for the better part of at least the past decade, Type A behavior has been our *de facto* model. The workaholic has become a cultural icon; moreover, with the workweek creeping back to levels of half a century ago, all-job-all-the-time can be necessary just to hang onto a job. The TINS generation – two incomes, no sex – is the matrimonial ideal. The hard-driving, work-around-the-clock, make-your-first-million-before-you're-thirty entrepreneur is our new-born prince. We're expected, all of us, to "get ours." We expect to, too.

Of course we'll put in more hours. *Sure* we'll make home an extension of the office, and be ready to rumble whenever the cell-phone or pager summons (*if you're not there, make sure to leave word where you are!*). Hey, it's a lean-and-mean, dog-eat-dog world out there.

Unfortunately, it's easy to lose sight of the *why* in trying to accomplish the *what*. What we know, *really know*, is important gets pushed into the background as other priorities move up. No wonder we're about as obsessed, insensitive, ill-mannered, worn out and judgmental as people can be without bashing each others' heads in... although the bashing-in has been getting more common all the time.

When I'm elected ruler of the universe, I'm going to outlaw blame and judgment. I'm not talking about conscience, that's something else and still the handiest tool yet for sorting out right from wrong. But pointing fingers at others with less than a constructive tone and arrogantly announcing that, *of course, you didn't do it as well as I could...* well, *disparaging* and *divisive* are perhaps the nicest terms that could apply.

We invest so much in making our self look good, to both ourselves and others. Ego is the name for it, and it's another of our mixed bags. Ego is a sort of immune system for the mind, protecting us from the ill effects of stress and anxiety. This classic two-edged sword, when it's cutting the other way, can misguide, deceive and lie to us in its self-inflating quest. The disease is self-consumption, the state of being self-consumed – no relation to the consumption brought on by night vapors that made maidens grow sallow and waste away a century ago.

Our self-consumption throws up a screen of ego that leaves us all but blind to what we're doing and how we come off. If we're not looking, how will we know? A friend or loved one might try to say something, give us a heads-up, but the self-consumed being will seldom take it to heart; indeed, the messenger will usually be blamed. As my partner in this book likes to point out, religions all seem to agree on one thing: *the problem. It's ego.* You – *I* – get in our own way.

From the East comes a metaphor about ego that is both simple and direct. Think of yourself as a lamp, they say, not the electric kind, but the old oil lamp complete with tall glass chimney. Since it's naturally meant to produce light, there's a flame inside. The flame is the spirit, the soul, humanity, a spark of the cosmic, a fragment of the divine.

As the lamp burns and produces light, carbon quickly clouds the chimney. Ignore it too long and light no longer shines through. Ego, of course, is the soot, which ultimately blacks out the divine energy inside. The antidote is a sort of perpetual spiritual housecleaning that scrubs away excess ego... not exactly a commonplace activity for most of us.

I know a surgeon who is a superb technician, one of the best I've ever seen. His techniques are near-flawless, and his ability to solve problems with the "knife and fork," dazzling. I would let him operate on me or any member of my family in a minute.

Yet his compulsion to be the best has driven him to believe nobody else can do it right. His behavior is judgment-filled. He makes little attempt to hide his feelings. If you imagine that the mere mention of his name in some hospital circles is enough to provoke anger and generate real stress, you're on the money.

Judging by our own sets of rules is not the stuff love, or healthy relationships, are made of.

If you accept my premise that to serve and love others is to foster connectedness in the world, then the really successful people *build* relationships, not tear them down. From talk shows to the halls of government, we haven't gotten that message too well.

I had a patient who taught me this clearly. Grant Gordon was a man who died in his 30's of lymphoma after a lengthy and painful battle. He was a wonderful friend and frequent participant in support groups I ran for the terminally ill. To everyone else who knew him, Grant was special. He loved others and it showed, in a very sincere and special way. What a wonderful model he was!

He lay in his hospital bed, thin, racked with pain and aware of his inevitable fate, as we had a private conversation a few weeks before he died. Like so many friends in the support group, Grant was a great teacher. I truly wanted to understand his "secret."

"How have you had the courage to keep such a bright outlook on life in the face of so much pain?"

My friend replied, "I never allowed myself the luxury of believing that fear was real."

Here was a man, much like Morrie Schwartz of Mitch Albom's *Tuesdays With Morrie*, who understood life. Yet I found myself doubting what he had just said.

"Everybody gets afraid, Grant," I said. "If you don't, you're being unrealistic."

Unrealistic. That's a great word we doctors use to help people face their problems.

"You don't understand," he said. "I'm not talking about that kind of fear, of the inevitable or the unknown. I'm speaking about the fear that is the opposite of love."

I've heard since that conversation that a good mnemonic for fear is "false evidence appears real." Grant saw fear as a lie, a prevarication. So if fear is a lie, then love is the truth, according to Grant. And he was right. The superabundance of negativity that brings down relationships arises from being afraid. Anger, bullying, insensitivity, judgmentalism, resentment – who doesn't know these on a first-name basis? They all come from the person who is afraid.

To refuse to reach out to another and truly love them, to deny the connection that relationship can bring, arises from fear of rejection. That's so old as to be a cliché – the jilted lover, for example, or partner in a bad marriage, who refuses to put the heart at risk again. They're the personification of Mark Twain's famous cat – the one who, after sitting on a hot stove, would never sit on a hot stove again... or on a cold one, either. We hate pain, especially when it's us on the receiving end. We avoid it by not opening ourselves to the possibility. We reject connecting with others from fear of getting hurt.

St. Exupery in *The Little Prince* tells what love is: "Love is my leading you back to whom you really are." No control, just freedom. Giving others the freedom to be themselves, without fear or anger or censure or belittlement. That's love. It's love that doesn't require romance or sainthood to give

You get back when you give, the old saw still cuts keenly. *What goes around comes around, you reap what you sow, you make your own bed,* and to those in the Eastern world, *karma.* To become fully human and to experience our personhood, to understand what true wellness is all about, are all mightily anchored in loving relationships.

In response to diabolic disaster we have seen love and its power as maybe never before in our lives. The window opened, showing us example after example of loving relationships, of people helping people simply because they can. The cost of that lesson has been terrible, yes. We can't undo it, but we can learn from it.

Find the meaning, then live it like you mean it. Extend love to self and others. Consciously make it an integral part of your life, and before long, conscious effort won't be necessary. Love comes in many forms, and each enobles. It can be something as dramatic as a firefighter risking life to rescue another, or something as mundane as a passerby stopping to help a person who lives on the street.

Here are thoughts on building connections:

1. Forgive. Develop a short memory when it comes to others' failings. Forgiving others' shortcomings becomes the quickest way to forgive ourselves.

2. Keep learning. Others are the best source for the knowledge we need to fully know ourselves.

3. Thank someone who has enriched your day. Gratitude and graciousness are the keys to loving and serving relationships.

4. Overlook flaws. Others know their own flaws, or will in time. Don't use the truth as a weapon to wound.

5. Encourage the discouraged. Life is invariably a team effort, and that means reaching out to others. Do it, and others will reach out to you.

We are at our human best when we're serving others.

4

Finding Meaning

In the corner of Pennsylvania where I live, one of the familiar rituals of summer is a weekend at the Jersey shore. From Friday through early Saturday afternoon, there's a steady stream of traffic as the Philadelphia megalopolis, the whole eastern half of the state, and large pieces of New York and New Jersey migrate to the beach.

Most of those people also have to get home Sunday afternoon. Of course, only the most prudent souls pack up and leave early to beat the crowd. More hold out to the bitter end. Then, within a couple of hours, hundreds of thousands of people begin the westward migration. As Philadelphia nears, drivers find themselves shunted onto a single bridge that carries travelers from New Jersey to Pennsylvania.

The traffic jams are legendary. And on this particular Sunday evening, I'm some of the stuff that legends are made of. On the bridge, a half dozen cars or so ahead, a fender-bender has brought all to a standstill.

Ever watch people in traffic? I do. Since we'll be here for a while, I turn off the ignition and start looking around. Next to me is a guy venting his frustration on the steering wheel and dashboard. He's pounding his fists and mouthing expletives. He turns to sees me looking at him. With the bravado that only comes from too many beers or sitting behind a 3,000 pound piece of machinery, he salutes me with a decisive upward thrust of his middle finger.

I hit the lock button and snap my head straight ahead. But you can't escape 'em – in front of me there's another one: a middle- aged man in the family sedan, wife and kids within, leaning on the horn. Nobody's going anywhere. There are five cars in front of him and, beyond that, the two disabled vehicles and chunks of twisted metal.

That irritates the daylights out of the guy behind me. He sticks his head out the window and starts yelling to the guy on the horn – who couldn't hear above the noise, anyway. God is a funny guy, again. Among all this confusion, frustration and rage, He decides to hold a workshop.

Two cars up and one car over, there's a decades-old Chevy. If cars had diseases, this piece of four-wheeled pathology would soon be taking the final exit on the Great Expressway. The rear bumper, held up by a piece of coat hanger, hangs at a ten-degree angle. A loud, pounding bass pours from the car causing everything within a fifty-foot radius to vibrate. You'd swear that the old Chevy was expanding and contracting with the beat.

I crane my neck to get a look at the young rowdies in the car, except my preconception is off base. The sole occupant is an old guy, easily seventy-five or eighty, wearing a baseball cap and grooving to the music. Head thrown back and eyes closed, he might be an arthritic Ray Charles, wagging and bopping and belting out the words, mostly out of synch. The music's so loud and his activity so bizarre that everyone around him has to look…and starts to laugh.

A young woman gets out of a nearby car. She pounds on the old guy's window – and again, finally rousting him from his revel. They talk for a few seconds, and the most amazing thing happens: the old guy gets out of the car, and he and the young woman *dance!*

Another couple gets out of their car and joins in. Here on the deck of a bridge named for poet Walt Whitman – what a fitting place, honoring the bard who celebrated the ordinary like few others ever have – we're having a block party. The odd couple does a little jitterbug as others leave their vehicles to clap, cheer them on and join in.

I'll bet everybody there remembers this little incident long after memories of the traffic jam and all else from their weekend are forgotten. Did the old guy and his young "date" seize the opportunity and make the most of it? Believe it!

I'm reminded of Morrie Schwartz in Mitch Albom's book, *Tuesdays With Morrie*. The only picture in the entire volume is Morrie dancing *alone*. A sort of urban American Zorba the Greek, he's filled with the joy of the moment he's experiencing.

What a wonderful way to deal with a moment of confusion and inconvenience.

Now for the rest of the story: the damaged cars are finally cleared and traffic starts moving. Near the toll booth I notice that the character in the beat-up car is right in front of me. I'm close enough to read the faded sticker on the cockeyed bumper: it says, *"Celebrate the Ordinary!"*

Talk about somebody who walks the walk and talks the talk. This man owns the truth. He *knows*. He used his considerable imagination not only to solve a problem, but to launch a celebration... a celebration of the *moment*. I think he did considerably more than celebrate the ordinary, too: he made the ordinary *extraordinary*.

When we inevitably fall into more-or-less ordinary lives, we yearn for something extraordinary to break the routine. That yearning is serious, too. We're seldom as creative as the guy in the beat-up Chevy, but we're willing to take high-stakes risks to jumpstart our oh-so-routine everydays. Switching jobs, having a midlife crisis, taking up skydiving, drinking too much, joining the Army (or the circus in the old days), "workaholism," having an affair, micromanaging our kids, gambling – they're some of a legion of time-honored means of beating the humdrum.

We're not only easily bored, we're fickle. How quickly our

attitudes are adjusted when bad times hit. *Then* we yearn for the ordinary and realize how wonderful it really is. If the tragedy is bad enough, we probably would give anything to have our wonderful monotony back, just the way it was. Suddenly, the ordinary becomes extraordinary.

I remember a World War II vet speaking about his homecoming from the Pacific a few weeks after VJ Day. For nearly two-and-a-half years he had hopped from the hell of one island invasion to another.

"You dream a lot when you're in something like that," he explained. "I had the same dream for years. It was dinner at home, always fried chicken and apple pie, and then going into the parlor with everybody to listen to the radio. I'd take a hot bath, drive into town, and meet a girl at the movies. I could smell the popcorn."

For weeks after he actually was back home he would pinch himself – "just checking that I hadn't died and gone to heaven." For weeks he didn't want to sleep because he was afraid of waking up and finding his dream wasn't real.

Would he say without hesitation that there's magic in the ordinary? And he also lived his life in a way that sought to make every day a celebration of the ordinary.

The ordinary should be extraordinary, because that's the "house" we live in most of the time. We can't live life from vacation to vacation, or weekend to weekend, or great victory to great victory. Well, we *can*, but what a terrible waste of all that's in between.

Tragedies walk right up and – *pow!* – deliver a shock. When they have our attention, they remind how precious and tenuous life is. I'll sometimes ask people what they would do differently if they had just three months to live? Their answers tell right away who's living life and who's just getting through it. If the list is more than a few items long, it's time to start making serious changes, and now.

To Buddhists, living the moment is at the very center of their practice. "The past is a memory," goes a famous Buddhist quotation, "the future is but an illusion." The only moment we have is the moment we're living.

Life isn't a rehearsal. *Live the life you'd live if you had only three months.*

THE ISLAND-NATION of Taiwan suffered what the *Taipei Times* called "its worst disaster in recent memory" on September 21, 1999. A massive, 7.3-force earthquake rocked the island, leaving some 2,000 dead, 4,000 injured, and many others homeless. To a country the size of Taiwan, the extent of the tragedy was numbing. Virtually every Taiwanese had a relative or friend killed, injured or left homeless.

Their reaction was remarkable on two counts. Here are excerpts from the *Taipei Times* report of September 22, *Finding unity in adversity:*

"Almost the entire population of the country was startled... and their anxiety turned to shock as reports of the extent of damage began to come in.

"The deepest impression, at least in the immediate aftermath, has been the way in which people throughout the island have pulled together in response to the calamity.... In short, the tragedy has demonstrated the fundamental strength and maturity of Taiwanese society in the face of crisis.

"Police, fire and rescue services, joined by the military and large numbers of neighborhood volunteers, got to work swiftly....

"Taiwan's political leaders, at both the central and local levels, and from all parties, have also displayed... words and deeds [that] mark a refreshing change from the vicious backbiting....

"The expressions of concern from the international political community... are gratifying...."

The parallels to how America responded to the terrorist attacks are striking... but then, not really. The world over, people suffer, work to overcome it, and act in extraordinary ways. People are much more alike than different. The story goes on:

"...but we must also remember, in the future, to step up our humanitarian assistance efforts to other countries in good times. One never knows when one's generosity will be repaid or by whom.

"During the period of cleanup and reconstruction, we hope that all Taiwanese people can continue to build on the foundation that has been laid on this first day. The creation of a model for national participation and cooperation would be the best gift this tragedy can bestow, and the best way its victims can be honored."

Another Taiwanese newspaper, the *United Daily News*, similarly remarked on the selflessness of people and the restraint of politicians, closing with the hope that "we can quickly recover from this catastrophe, with a new understanding of our future course."

Those closing paragraphs are, to me, truly remarkable. Keep in mind that just about everybody in Taiwan was personally affected by the quake. Yet only hours after the tragic event, there already are calls to look beyond the suffering and find meaning. There is wisdom in those remarks: moving forward with a heightened sense of involvement and cooperation certainly would be "the best gift this tragedy can bestow, and the best way its victims can be honored."

Finding meaning in the tragedy... it's not meaning as in *why it happened*, but *wisdom* —meaning that can work *meaningful change*. What better way to honor the victims than with such a legacy?

THE TIME IT TAKES to recover from a loss is never "standard." Some people seem to bounce back in days, although much of that is the show of a stiff upper lip. Very few will really manage such a speedy recovery from a severe loss. Others appear to ingest their mourning, to feed on it and make it the very center of their lives. But most who go through the cycle of grief, beginning with denial and moving through the predictable stages, do reach the plateau of acceptance. They become more or less "normal" again, doing normal things in normal ways.

"Getting back to normal," we were told in the weeks following September 11, is our patriotic chore. Our political, business and civic leaders started saying as much just a day or two after the September 11 attack. Since then, they've been repeating as a mantra that to do less is to admit defeat. Their message, a very valid one, speaks to the need to get the nation "running again."

But sometimes the problem is that things *do* return to *the way they were*. Getting up and running again doesn't have to mean *deja vu all over again*. I believe that if we can extract the message we have been allowed to see in tragedy, we can consciously choose to live a *normal* that is not an unedited copy of yesterday.

Immediately after the terrorist attacks, crime of just about every description declined – not only in New York City, but over much of the country. Even the bad guys, it seemed, had been softened by the public terror. How long did this holiday from crime last? It was a mere blip on our screen. In less than two weeks, crime was creeping back up to pre-September 11 levels. Normal certainly was returning.

If that's the normal we return to, we're as much as admitting that there *is no meaning* to the experience at all... only pain. So often we look at painful experiences as we look at our everydays: as obstacles to get around, barriers to get past, problems to slog through. We forget why we're here: to learn and to love. In those purposes we're different from all other beings. They make us human.

It's sometimes said that God gives us trials and adversity so we do learn. Others say, no, adversity isn't God's doing at all, but rather, man's – that "free will thing" of ours has always been a bit of a problem. Still others say it's neither, but an organized evil force in the world – Satan, if we put a face on it. We can argue, philosophize and believe one or the other, but the precise *why* of it all is another candidate for the box we mark *answerless*, at least in this lifetime.

I do believe there is a reason for all of the pain and struggle. We were put on earth to learn something. If everything were perfect, we would have no opportunity to elevate our spirits through the events we experience.

I was on a flight from Jacksonville to Atlanta several years ago, trying to make a connection to O'Hare in Chicago. I had just delivered a talk to a large hospice organization, and was headed to a similar presentation in northern Illinois. I was tired but satisfied, enjoying a sense of accomplishment for a job well done.

I boarded a 767 jetliner that was brand-spanking new – it even smelled new. I mentioned it to the flight attendant as I took my seat, and she told me this was the fourth flight this plane was making after its shakedown. There was something reassuring about that. In the news lately were disturbing reports that cost-cutting airlines were flying planes well beyond the hours they were designed for.

I watched the spectacular sunset at 30,000 feet sink into a beautiful and clear twilight. The trip was to be about forty minutes.

It turned out to be much longer.

If you fly a lot you come to know that speed, descent and wing configuration are pretty much the same for every aircraft, new or not. They weren't the same here. Our approach speed for an airspace as crowded as Atlanta's was much too fast. At our altitude, there should have been signs of flaps or spoilers moving. They were ominously still. Something was very wrong.

The captain came on the intercom: "Folks, we're having difficulty with the hydraulics to our flaps. We cannot control our speed properly and need to get out of this airspace and circle until we can figure out our problem. We'll get back to you."

Get back to me? Where are you going? Wherever it was, I wanted to go, too! Suddenly things are not so ordinary. Panicky looks replace the usual sleepy boredom. Airphones start popping from their cradles as people begin calling loved ones, some even saying their final good-byes. Flight attendants trot up and down the aisle trying to be reassuring, but their faces, too, betray concern.

My first reaction was a twinge of anger. I was angry because I had so much to do yet with my life, and being trapped in a racing bullet of aluminum a couple of miles above the ground wasn't one of them. People go through a period of denial and anger in bad situations, as I was, but in a situation like this you move quickly from denial to terror. The root emotion is *scared*. What your fear drives you to do ultimately determines the lesson you learn and the meaning you glean.

We circled... and circled... and circled, for two hours, burning off fuel for the emergency landing ahead. I decided to take out a legal pad and write. Writing has a calming effect for me, pulling into play the part of the mind that's analytical and rational. As part of the bargaining I was doing with God – a lot of us are eager to do some serious horse trading when facing our own mortality – I started listing all the things I would do if God would only permit me to survive this situation.

I guess I could have talked about curing cancer, feeding the poor in Ethiopia, or making a religious pilgrimage, but once the terror of the moment passes, those grand and global promises tend not to make it into reality. I decided instead to write what I thought was reasonable, doable. I listed such things such as:

Next time I'm at a baseball game I will really make an effort to catch a foul ball.

I'm going to be ever-present to my children when they want to share something with me.

I'm going to stop at the park I pass every day to savor the happy sounds of children playing, and experience their joy.

My list had 101 items by the time we made our emergency

approach – you can tell I was serious about earning as many bargaining chips as I could. We could see emergency vehicles lining the runway as we assumed our tucked-in emergency landing position. We were coming in faster than anyone of us would have liked and there were some frightened screams as the plane bounced onto the runway, but we were OK, we landed safely.

As we collectively regained our composure and began to deplane, reactions were varied. Some passengers were saying they would never fly again, some were thanking everyone from God to the flight attendants, and one absolute ass was complaining about missing his connection. The ass obviously learned nothing, and would go right back to working on his heart attack and making everybody around him miserable.

I decided to put one item on my list into action immediately. As I left the aircraft, I thanked every crew member I could find, personally and sincerely, making eye-to-eye contact as I did. On my list was thanking someone every day afterward for a well-done job, and this seemed like a very good place to start.

As of today I've scratched off seventy items from my now-tattered list. And I intend to do the same to the other thirty-one, one of which is still catching that baseball.

There's often no explanation for the why things happen. They just do. People get cancer, planes sometimes fall out of skies, marriages break up, unsuspecting people are murdered by terrorists. If we're lucky we learn lessons that help us avoid these tragedies in the future. Doing that can help those involved, or left behind, move on with a new knowledge and perspective.

Why is a question born of anger, but there comes a time that we need to move past the anger and the unanswerable and get to the *how* of it. What we really desire – and what we can really use – is not an answer for the unfathomable, but an answer to *what is to become of us*?

How can I survive this tragedy? *How* can I go on without this loved one in my life? *How* can I adapt to this new direction my life has taken? My patients who heal and gain mature insight into their life-threatening difficulties have shown me that *these* are the questions that count.

One such young woman is Maria. Her story begins when she was a senior medical student at Georgetown University. At the age of twenty-eight, less than two months from graduation, a drunk driver hit her as she crossed Wisconsin Avenue in D.C.

"I just stepped from the curb and he hit me," she told me. "And in that slow-motion, strangely detached view of what was happening, I knew that I wasn't going to die. I knew something far worse was going to happen."

Maria hit the asphalt and broke her neck. She was now a quadriplegic. "People had to haul my paralyzed body from place to place. I could do little more than talk, breathe, swallow and shrug my shoulders." And she raged at what had happened to her.

She was transferred to a rehabilitation center, and she continued to be angry at everyone – her doctors, nurses, family, therapists, anyone interested in helping. She was angry most of all at God. "All I ever wanted to be was a doctor, and this is what you do to me. And if you didn't do it, why didn't you stop it, why did you let this happen to me?" Like Elie Weisel's tribunal in the concentration camp, she found God guilty.

And then, someone penetrated her anger and reached her. This fellow patient, a teenager, had been in a driving accident that left him a quadriplegic. He had seen her anger and lashing out. After all, she didn't much care about keeping it a secret.

"Maria, if God wanted you to be a basketball player," he said one day, "He would have made you seven feet tall and given you the moves of a Michael Jordan. But instead, God *let you – didn't make you* – he let you become a quad. Now, why don't you become the best person with quadriplegia you can become, or *die,* 'cause otherwise, you're really wasting a lot of other people's time." Talk about a dose of reality.

As she thought about his words, she began to realize he was right. "And I began to heal," Maria said. "Slowly I came to realize life still held hope and goals. I taught myself how to type at a keyboard holding a pencil in my mouth. I learned how to draw, too, holding crayons and then a paintbrush in my mouth. And know what? Even though people have to haul my body from place to place, I'm still worthwhile." She has gone on to become an active figure in the campaign to curb drunk driving.

Life goes on with or without you. And living is not an elective, it is a required course. We learn one way or the other, and if we don't, perhaps we're bound to keep repeating the course until we finally get a passing grade.

ALTHOUGH DIFFERENT in scale from the subsequent terrorist attacks, the Oklahoma City bombing was certainly no less a tragedy. Until September 11, it ranked as America's worst terrorist attack.

One of the victims in the Alfred P. Murrah Federal Building was a twenty-four-year-old woman who died doing a small act of kindness. If she had stayed in her office at the rear of the building, she would have survived the explosion. She didn't have to, but the young lady had gone to the lobby to lead a confused man, unable to speak English, to her office to complete a Social Security application. While she and her client were in the lobby, the front of the building crumbled in the blast.

Her father, a Lutheran minister, was devastated by the loss of his only child. The next several months he mourned, turning much of his grief into hate for Timothy McVeigh, mastermind of the bombing. The pastor's Sunday sermons had evolved from testaments of love and forgiveness to angry tirades on justice. Depressed and terribly despondent, he came to realize what was happening. Consumed by hate, he was becoming like the misdirected murderer.

Committing to getting beyond his anger, he told himself he had to go let go of *why* of the senseless act and move on to the *how*. He eventually was able to contact MacVeigh's father. He, likewise, was suffering tremendously for his son's murder of 163 innocent lives. What must the father of a Timothy McVeigh feel? By all accounts he is a good man, as perplexed as anyone else by his son's behavior. The pastor and the father met. The father of the victim told the father of the bomber that he forgave his son. And then, the pastor tried to console the man in his tremendous grief, sorrow, guilt and anger. It took great courage and compassion.

On the well-televised day of MacVeigh's execution, while the press interviewed those who mostly demanded justice and death in return for the murders, this minister sat and prayed with MacVeigh's dad. In a very private place, they consoled one another for their mutual losses, each moving beyond the reasons to the lessons – to the new morning, the new beginnings that had to come.

MANY BOOKS DEAL well with handling grief and loss. I think perhaps that most important in a time of national crisis is to *get past the unanswerable why*. When you do that, you open yourself to the truth you can own. In the end, that lesson comes from looking inward. It is very simple and very profound.

Some "get it" quickly. Others are considerably slower on the uptake. Some never get it. The timetable for growth varies from individual to individual.

I had a young friend who had leukemia. Jason, eight years old, required special medical care and for six weeks was a patient at Children's Hospital of Philadelphia. When he felt well enough to sit up, he would pass the time drawing and finger painting, his favorite things to do. The first picture he drew was a tall, svelte man with a full head of curly, brown hair. He labeled his artwork "Dr. Leo," and sent it off to me.

It arrived one Saturday morning with a little note scrawled in a childish hand. The picture was hysterical, since *svelte* and *full head of hair* aren't things you would normally associate with me. When I proudly showed them the portrait of *me*, my children gave me the classic teenage roll of the eyes and a "Yeah, right!" Anyway, that picture stayed up on the old GE Foodmaster for many months.

The note was as wise as it was touching. "Dr. Leo," it began. "My daddy told me. There is no yesterday, there is no tomorrow. I should worry only about *to-now.*"

To-now. That's where we live, in the moment we have. That's where we apply the lessons we learned from turning the *whys* to *hows.*

HERE'S A SIMPLE, or even simplistic, plan for healing. Adjectives notwithstanding, it works, whether the pain is one person's very private grief or a tragedy that affects a nation.

1. Embrace the grief. Mourning for a loss prompts an understanding of not only its importance in your life, but an appreciation for all else you have.

2. Look inward. The answers and the wisdom reside in the part of each of us inhabited by the divine. Don't be afraid to find that part of yourself that shows your true nature and direction.

3. Let go of fear, use love's power. The power is tremendous. Fear, not hatred, is love's opposite.

4. Connect with others. The moment you understand your own sense of worth and direction, you'll know who everyone else is and can become. Connect with that *in them*. It's as close as a touch, a gentle word, an act of kindness.

5. Find meaning. Understanding begins with recognizing that some things have no earthly explanation. Let them go, and look instead for the wisdom that waits to be found.

AT THE END OF the day the sun will set, and just as surely, rise again on a new day. The morning always brings the same question: what do we do with it?

Each of us chooses how we answer. Or we don't choose, risking a default that's "more of the same" at best.

In time there will be a memorial in metal or stone to those who have perished. That's as it should be. But *even more enduring*, perhaps, would be a *living memorial*, built on a foundation of *the possible* that we've been allowed to see.

Far from the dreamy-eyed impracticalities we've been conditioned to see them as, inclusiveness, cooperation, service and love just may be the cure for what has ailed us for too long. We can each be that living memorial if we choose to be.

There couldn't be a more complete healing.

Epilog

The seashore has always been a special place. When I was a kid, our whole family would vacation there. It was a wonderful time then, and a source of wonderful memories today.

It's still a favorite place where the entire family likes to gather to relax and reunite, and has been especially important to my mother, who turns eighty this year. She is a strong and very fit woman who lost her husband, my dad, to cancer about three years ago. She misses him terribly. They were best friends and lovers for more than fifty-seven years.

My dad loved the seashore almost as much as loved his family. He totally enjoyed walking the beach, fishing, jumping the waves and enjoying his children and grandchildren. I always picture Dad in our happiest times surrounded by the family he loved, drinking a Michelob on a porch overlooking the Atlantic. We often talk about how pop would make all of us feel happy with his endless well of jokes, or the surprises he would bring from the shops down the road from the beach house where we always stayed.

I cherish those dozens of summers I shared with him and the rest of my family. I miss that and I miss him, and although we still gather at the beach, it's just not the same.

Last August we vacationed there, and as we were talking about Dad, a beautiful butterfly seemed to appear out of nowhere to land on the table next to my mother and daughter. It was unusual – brown with deep yellow and orange spots, very unlike the monarchs so prevalent there in the late summer. What kind was it? Nobody knew, we hadn't come across the likes of it before. It just sat there, appearing to listen to the conversation.

When my daughter went to shoo it away, it flew a few feet and then landed again in the same spot, as if stubbornly refusing to be left out of the conversation. When our talking was through, it lingered briefly and then flitted away. It was strange, but not extraordinary. Although we all probably thought the same thought, if only briefly, nobody was ready to call it anything more than coincidence.

Several weeks later, on a glorious September day, my mother sat at her kitchen table looking out the window. She was thinking of Dad and how he would work in the driveway just beyond the window, or wash the car there. For many years, on days much like this, she would call to him to take a break and join her for a cup of coffee.

And then she was startled to see a beautiful brown butterfly with yellow and orange details on the windowsill. It seemed to just sit looking at her. My mother immediately thought of that other day a few weeks before, when she also had been thinking of Dad and "that" butterfly had appeared. Just as suddenly as it arrived it flew off .

Shortly after that – actually, it was the week of September 11 – my mother made a routine visit to her mother's gravesite near Philadelphia. Then she visits my dad's, just a few hundred feet beyond. She placed some early fall flowers there and prayed silently for the man she loved so much and for the victims of that week's tragedy.

When she opened her eyes, the first thing she saw was the flowers she had placed. There, among the profusion of mums, was a brown butterfly with intense yellow and orange spots. It just sat there. Mom bent over to pick it up, but the butterfly lifted off with two gigantic flaps of its wings and landed on my mother's arm. She stood there with tears in her eyes looking at this beautiful creation of nature staring back.

Butterflies are wonderful pieces of nature's artistry. They

represent in so many ways the renewal and revival nature brings to earth. And to my mother and the rest of our family, they also represent a life transformed. They are a sign of the next great adventure.

I believe there are no coincidences. *God-incidences,* maybe, but nothing that happens without purpose. It certainly is "right" to look for meaning in the tragedies that affect all of us, whether at a very personal or a global level. I might suggest we look, too, for meaning in God-incidences that help light our paths.

My mother would suggest we all look for butterflies.

An Excerpt From Our Upcoming Volume...

Look for the next volume by Drs. Leo Frangipane and Gary Kunkelman, tentatively scheduled for spring 2002. Its working title: Remind Me Again Why I Took This Job*, a look at how to achieve personal healing and wholeness in a hectic world.*

Coincidences can be wonderful things, even if we casually dismiss them on the grounds of familiarity. Well even go so far as to attach a familiar first name, "Just" – "Just Coincidence." Of course, being on a first name basis suggests we know all about coincidence. Thinking that we do – that it's all "just coincidence" – helps us write it off.

I invite you to think of coincidences as doors that swing open for brief seconds, offering quick entry to a place we'd seldom reach by our own conscious effort. Think of coincidences as a moment when self and an opportunity collide. In their illuminating flash, if we're quick enough to pick up on it, we might glimpse a life-changing new path. The phone call I received on that July day in 1985 was just such a coincidence.

In retrospect, you'd think a life-changing event should be announced with a bit more drama and fanfare: booming voices from a cloud, the all-illuminating flash of light, or at least a modest roll of drums or flourish of trumpets. But enlightenment doesn't always dawn as dramatically as we think it should. I've got to believe that what mine lacked in drama was compensated for, at least in part, by the packaging: I don't know too many people whose enlightenment was in the form of a diseased organ.

"I've got a hot gallbladder for you," the telephone voice said.

It was my partner, a surgeon in the practice, and his voice wasn't one I longed to hear. My day had been exhausting. His cut-to-the-chase hello told me it wasn't through.

"I put it on your schedule," he said, although I didn't need to be told. I was on call, the gallbladder was mine. I asked if *it* had a name, and jotting it down, pulled myself up for another round.

I grumbled, of course – that had become part of my act – yet I could feel the adrenaline build on the short drive to the hospital. Some people get their highs jumping out of airplanes or closing the big deals; for me, the rush – the only rush left in my job – was the O.R.

Even though I'd done it thousands of times, surgery was *magic*. The broken body would be wheeled in and, *abracadabra!*, wheeled out, whole. Then I could take my bows, the magician who put the sawed-in-half lady back together again. Here there was no Monday morning. Time didn't matter. Here seemed to be the answer to why I took this job in the first place.

As the "hot gallbladder" had come in through the ER not much earlier, the patient file I picked up when I got to the hospital hadn't yet fattened to novella size. That was a small blessing. Unscheduled surgeries always mean a time crunch, and this one was no exception. "We need to get the patient asleep and done," the nurse-supervisor commanded, "there's an emergency heart waiting to go in."

I maneuvered into surgical scrubs, at the same time leafing through the chart. Nothing out of the ordinary – a garden-variety gallbladder.

The surgery *was* totally routine, and I headed for bed with the satisfaction of having done my usual workmanlike job. The hot gallbladder's recovery was equally smooth. After two days in the hospital, about half the normal stay, she was well enough to go home. That I hadn't seen her during her brief hospitalization wasn't unusual; in a group practice the partners will take turns handling hospital rounds, and my partner had rounds during her stay.

It wasn't especially unusual, either, that I didn't make an immediate connection two weeks later, when I pulled her chart from the gray plastic pocket outside the exam room. Staring at the name, I tried to translate it into a diseased organ. That I had never seen the woman upright and conscious didn't help with a mental picture.

A glance inside the manila folder yielded the omniscience a surgeon's supposed to have: *of course, the hot gallbladder, two-week post-op exam.*

Breezing into the exam room in my authoritative, business-like professional manner, I automatically asked the patient how she was, hardly hearing the answer as I took aim for the right upper quadrant of her abdomen and the incision. I flipped up the hospital gown, knowing a quick look at the wound would tell me all I needed to know.

Years later as I replayed this scene, it struck me that not even Bill Clinton could do what I did: yank and tug at a woman's clothing, undress her to get to the portion of the anatomy I was intent on, and then *charge* her for it.

"Excuse me," she said politely, "but who *are* you?"

What? I couldn't believe she was asking that.

Who am I? Part of me was silently replying that *I'm the one who worked this magic, who painstakingly removed the diseased organ, and who, hello, saved your life.* Wouldn't medicine be wonderful without patients!

Yet I knew, in those same few moments, why I was angry: *I didn't have a good answer.*

Suddenly, my restless feeling that the practice of medicine had somehow gotten away from me was much less vague. It came into focus: *you really are doing something wrong, Leo,* the interior messenger was saying. That was an indictment, not an observation. With the high stakes, you can't be wrong and succeed in this game.

This lesson of professional infallibility is implanted the first day of clinical rotations in medical school, then pounded in again at every stage of training. Be perfect. That's the minimum acceptable standard. Obsessive as it may sound, the goal is lofty, even necessary, because there really *is* so little room for error. The downside of striving to be perfect is that we come to believe we are.

Who was I? Truly, *I didn't know any more.* There was no way this woman, this faceless object to me, could have known, either. We were perfect strangers. This magician had botched the trick, the whole act had gone wrong.

I looked at her for the first time – *really looked.* In her eyes, pale with years, I didn't see the patient I was trained to see: body, incision, chart, laboratory numbers. For the first time in years I saw a person. I saw her *self.* For a moment –I believe it to this day – I saw her *soul.*

Her simple, polite question summed up what I had lost…as a physician, and as a human being.

By the end of the week I announced I was leaving the practice. There had to be something besides hurried, impersonal, high-pressure medicine…dispassionate curing that seemed so distant from what medicine was supposed to be.

To Order by Mail

From Mourning to Mourning   _____ copies @$11 each   Total $_____
Two-cassette Book on Tape   _____ copies @$11 each   Total $_____
Save! Book & Tape Set   _____ copies @$20 each   Total $_____

If your order is $100 or more take a 20% discount now!

Merchandise Subtotal	$_____
S&H, $2 per item	$_____
PA residents add 6%	$_____
Total Enclosed	$_____

Name_____
Street_____
City_____ State_____ Zip_____
Phone_____ email_____

If you would like items sent in your name, please provide recipients' names, shipping addresses, and items and quantity to send.

Name_____
Street_____
City_____ State_____ Zip_____

Item: Book(s) #_____   Tape(s) #_____   Set(s) #_____

Name_____
Street_____
City_____ State_____ Zip_____

Item: Book(s) #_____   Tape(s) #_____   Set(s) #_____

Make checks payable to   **Leo G. Frangipane, M.D.**
Mail To: **Mourning to Morning Orders**
       P.O. Box 6923
       Wyomissing, PA 19610

Fax: 610-356-3477

Copies can be ordered from Dr. Leo's website: www.drleo.com

To Order by Mail

From Mourning to Mourning _____ copies @$11 each Total $_____
Two-cassette Book on Tape _____ copies @$11 each Total $_____
Save! Book & Tape Set _____ copies @$20 each Total $_____

If your order is $100 or more take a 20% discount now!

Merchandise Subtotal $_____
S&H, $2 per item $_____
PA residents add 6% $_____
Total Enclosed $_____

Name_____
Street_____
City_____ State_____ Zip_____
Phone_____ email_____

**If you would like items sent in your name, please provide recipients'
names, shipping addresses, and items and quantity to send.**

Name_____
Street_____
City_____ State_____ Zip_____

Item: Book(s) #_____   Tape(s) #_____   Set(s) #_____

Name_____
Street_____
City_____ State_____ Zip_____

Item: Book(s) #_____   Tape(s) #_____   Set(s) #_____

Make checks payable to   Leo G. Frangipane, M.D.
Mail To: Mourning to Morning Orders
P.O. Box 6923
Wyomissing, PA 19610

Fax: 610-356-3477

Copies can be ordered from Dr. Leo's website: www.drleo.com

If you would like to read more...

These books by Dr. Leo Frangipane are available at www.drleo.com. You can also order additional copies of *From Mourning to Morning* there, as well as the book on tape.

Touchstones and Wellsprings
An inspirational journey through the lives of people whose goal is not only to survive, but to live life to its fullest – even in the face of some of life's most trying times. It's warm, humorous, inspiring, motivational, meaningful and most of all, it's true. **$11.00**

More True Blue Tales
A collection of heart-rendering short stories in the motif of Chicken Soup for the Soul. One hundred tales that center on the journey of the human spirit. Makes you laugh, makes you cry... and will touch your life. **$11.00**

Audio Tapes

Touchstones and Wellsprings
Dr. Leo at his best. A full hour of his program presented live for the National Hospice Group. Storytelling as only he can do, in his own words, from the depth of his heart. **$6.95**

Focusing on the Right Stuff
Join Dr. Leo for 35 minutes of attitudinal adjustment. If you are what you eat, you are what you think! Especially good for people undergoing difficult times and stress. **$6.95**

Live, Life, Laugh, and Give
Highly popular four-tape set that's a blend of humor and health. Dr. Leo clowns and encourages you to take yourself lightly, as you take what you do seriously. Good for organizations undergoing stress of change; those dealing with aging or ill loved ones, and caregivers experiencing stress. Three full hours. **$24.95**

The Chicago Interviews
Another unique four-tape set. Two-and-a-half hour interview with the popular Chicago talk-show host Terri Murphy, as she explores with Dr. Leo the topics of health, wholeness and the meaning of life. Includes one of Dr. Leo's popular meditations. A most interesting and enlightening session you won't want to miss. **$24.95**

Will you help create a living history?

The attacks on America showed mankind at its worst as well as at its best. In the aftermath of the terrorists' carnage, ordinary people responded in extraordinary ways. Although few of these individuals seek publicity or personal gain, we believe these examples of the finest of the human spirit should be recorded. That's why historian Dr. Gary Kunkelman and Dr. Leo Frangipane have begun The America Attacked History Project.

Our goal is to create a clearinghouse to preserve this important information. We plan to donate these records to a university or historical repository that will make them available to future researchers, writers and historians. We are asking everyone with firsthand knowledge to help create this oral history for the future.

If you have personal knowledge of inspiring, heroic or loving acts arising from the attacks, or any acts and events that you believe will help create a full historical record, we invite you to send them to us. Small acts of caring can sometimes be as telling as great acts of heroism, so please don't edit out "the small things."

We have included several blank pages at the end of this book as a reminder of the stories that remain to be told. We invite you to fill them with your story. Then, please send us these pages or a copy of them. If you prefer, dictate your story onto an audio or even video cassette. So that we don't add to the large amount of misinformation already circulating, please send only information that you personally know to be true.

It's not imperative that you identify yourself, but if you choose to, it would help us tremendously: please include your name, email, telephone and mailing address. If possible, please include names and contact information for others who might have been involved. Similarly, if you know other people who might be able to provide additional information, please include their names and as much contact information as possible. In other words, we are seeking anything and everything that you think would help develop a complete historical archive memorializing those who died as well as recognizing those who helped.

Although we have no immediate plans to publish these stories, please know that they may be published by us or others at some future time and will become public records. Thank you in advance for your help.

Please send your information to
Oral History Project
PO Box 6115
Wyomissing, PA 19610

Or visit **www.drleo.com** and send it via the email feature there.